Full Surface Publishing

Demico Boothe is a bestselling author of several books. He is also an ex-prisoner who served over twelve years in federal prison. He is considered by many to be an expert on issues dealing with the African-American experience, African-American history, and the U.S. Prison Industrial Complex. He resides in Memphis, TN.

Richard Bovan, an ex-prisoner who served over ten years in prison, is now a successful self-made entrepreneur and motivational writer for the formerly and currently incarcerated. Richard is dedicated to helping curb crime and the high incarceration and recidivism rates of the U.S. criminal justice system and counsels ex-prisoners from all over the world on issues of mentality/lifestyle change, reentry, and achieving real success after incarceration.

The Smart Society's Guide
on How to Fight Crime, Reduce Recidivism, and Close Jails & Prisons

10 Things American Society Can Do to Decrease Crime and Increase Productivity Among Ex-Offenders

by

Demico Boothe and Richard Bovan

This book was published in Memphis, Tennessee,
the United States of America.
ISBN 979-8-9863171-0-6
Library of Congress Control Number: 2022939123

First Edition
This book can be purchased in bulk via the following
distributors: Ingram, Baker & Taylor, Barnes & Noble,
Amazon.com (U.S., U.K., & Canada) and Bertrams

This work is dedicated to all those
who have ever suffered
the indignity of imposed inequality.

1-5 Things American Society Can Do
to Decrease Crime and Increase Productivity
Among Ex-Offenders

6-10 Things American Society Can Do to Decrease Crime and Increase Productivity Among Ex-Offenders

"Wise progressivism and wise conservatism
go hand in hand."
- Theodore Roosevelt

"Building prisons to fight crime is like building
cemeteries to fight disease."
- Jack Levin

"It is said that no one truly knows a nation until
one has been inside its jails. A nation should not
be judged by how it treats its highest citizens,
but its lowest ones."
- Nelson Mandela

"If we should have white supremacy, we must
establish it by law—not by force or fraud."
- Alabama Constitutional Convention president
John B. Knox, 1901

Reducing Crime & Recidivism:
A Progressive Conservative Necessity Moving Forward

The recidivism rate, or return-to-prison rate, for ex-prisoners in America has been extremely high for a very long time. This, coupled with the fact that America has the largest prison system and highest incarceration rate in the world,[1] has created a crisis that now demands the full attention of us all. Much can and has been said about the causes of this crisis, but the focus of this book will be on a path forward that incorporates measures that truly can and will reduce crime and recidivism dramatically.

Both authors of this book have served over ten consecutive years inside prison and both of us have previously written books about the U.S. prison system and the rehabilitation and reacclimatization of former prisoners into society, mainly from the perspective of the "responsible" individual. Now, together, we will describe what we feel are necessary undertakings to dramatically reduce the prison population in America and lessen the return-to-prison rate for ex-prisoners, but from a societal and governmental point of view. In other words, there are some very specific things that we can do as a nation that will drastically reduce the massive burdens on society that are created by having such high crime rates and high recidivism rates among ex-prisoners.

As stated, currently, and consistently for the past several decades, the recidivism rate for ex-prisoners in America is and has been too high—around 70% overall.[2] This means that, within eight or nine years of being released, seventy out of every one hundred ex-prisoners are back behind bars. That stat is beyond ridiculous and a clear-cut sign of failed criminal justice social policy and practice. The high recidivism rate is largely responsible for the excessively large prison system as well as the high crime rate.[3] Judging by the past and present, America hasn't figured out how to get these issues under control. Many people think that this is because the politicians and courts are much more interested in catching, punishing and profiting off of criminals instead of seeking to institute the necessary preventative measures that lessen the likelihood of people committing crime.

As far as forming criminal justice policy is concerned, one of the main problems is that no one ever consults successful ex-prisoners about what exactly is needed to curtail this longstanding negative reality. Even when it comes to books on subjects dealing with the criminal justice system, most American institutions of higher learning choose to mainly utilize study materials that are put forth by degreed educators who typically have no real first-hand experience with the darker side of the criminal justice system. Data driven, imaginative ideas and efforts can only go so far and routinely miss the mark in pinpointing what needs to be done when it comes to this issue. Which is precisely why we, two ex-prisoners from two different parts of the country and from two different racial and ethnic backgrounds, decided to put together this book and add some real-life experience and a more complete bird's-eye view of the situation at hand. Our goal is simply to create a more thorough understanding of what can be done to successfully address the issues of high crime and high recidivism rates in America.

Over the past several decades, the political framers of American criminal justice policy have made a lot of mistakes. A whole lot. To the point that, precedents and judicial trends have now been firmly set into place that greatly undermine the overall health and progression of our society. Punitive approaches have become the primary go-to methods for creating and promoting social compliance with laws and law enforcement. To boot, policing has taken on a somewhat militant and adversarial posture more so than a protective and service posture, especially when it comes to minorities and the poor. Today, most black and Latino Americans feel that even routine, passing encounters with law enforcement personnel in the street are much more likely to be adversarial rather than good-natured.[4] America's prisons and jail systems have been severely overcrowded, mainly with minorities, for decades due to these approaches. For the past 30 years, America has not only had the world's largest prison population, but also the highest percentage of its citizenry behind bars of all nations.[5] And despite all the sporadic past and current convenient political talk about turning this situation around, the reality is that almost nothing is actually being done to pull things in the direction of real change.

The mix of educated opinions, double firsthand experiences and perspectives, and irrefutable facts that are presented in this book will give the reader a realistic ground-level blueprint of specific things that can be done to enact real and lasting change, which is drastic crime and recidivism reduction. We will show that not only are high crime levels in America preventable today, but that they have always been preventable. It comes down to the priorities of our society; whether or not we want to continue to normalize criminality to the point of enabling it by mainly focusing on punishment and incarceration, or do a bunch of things differently that will have the opposite effect. The ten things that we recommend in this book, if implemented, would surely reduce the overall crime rate by a large percentage and would probably reduce the current incarceration rate by 50% or more. We believe the recidivism rate would drop by about 50% as well, if not more. In each chapter, we will show exactly why we believe these things to be true.

Our general common themes are basically two-fold:

- Most crime in America for which people get incarcerated are, at the root, economic-based.[6] This means that, if assisted in the proper way, most people who get incarcerated and released would likely not reoffend. Incarceration does work as a social deterrent to crime for most people under normal circumstances, but that deterrence effect psychologically decreases when a person is economically desperate. Which directly explains why America's prisons and jails have always been mainly populated by poor people.

- For Americans that get incarcerated, jail and/or prison *should* be a place where they can get help getting their lives together, and to substantially subsidize that rehabilitative perspective is *not* an incentive for people to commit crime and get locked up. In fact, it's the smartest, most humane way to spend money that otherwise would be spent on other more punitive aspects of the criminal justice system.

As a nation, we have to be more willing to invest resources *in* our people and not just *on* our people; internal investment vs. external investment. There is a big difference between the two. External investment is often shallow, surface-level and short-lived, demanding constant revisiting and tweaking with only the potential for less-than-optimal results. While internal investment is more sophisticated, deep-reaching and long-lasting, with the potential for optimal results. Making internal investments in people usually takes care of everything an external investment could, and then some. Like teaching a man to fish vs. giving him fish to eat for dinner a few times; giving him fish for dinner a few times may be less taxing and time consuming on you but will do him no good in the weeks, months, and years to come when he gets hungry. But teaching him to fish, he'll not only eat for that day, but all days to come. Likewise, investing in the wholeness and wellbeing of a person, whether that person be an ex-prisoner or not but especially if so, will always yield better results than prioritizing social revenge against them with punishment and disenfranchisement, which is what we currently do.

Broken down into ten short chapters, these are our specific ideas on how we can institute change, for the overall betterment of our citizenry, and thus, our nation. America can and should do better where these issues are concerned, and it is our hope that we eventually will. We believe that a chain is only as strong as its weakest link. We also believe, as Nelson Mandela once so eloquently stated, that the truest measure of a nation is observed not by how it treats its rich and privileged, but how it treats its poor and disadvantaged.[7] And we do not believe that high crime rates are just a natural aspect of a capitalist social construct because there are too many examples and facts that disprove that. Again, the truth is, high crime rates in The United States of America are and always have been extinguishable and preventable. All it takes, all it has ever taken, is the right motivation and the right plan.

1

Make Ex-Prisoners Who've Paid Their Debts to Society Full Citizens Again by Outlawing Discrimination in Employment, Housing & Voting

Within the American criminal justice system, the core tenets of past-era American slavery are still very much alive and well. Forced free labor, forced family separation and harsh physical treatment aside, the most debilitating and damaging aspects of the American Slavery Experience were the accompanying race-based social discrimination, suppression and legal disenfranchisement. Since the ending of slavery, African-Americans have still had to continually face high levels of social and economic discrimination and disenfranchisement, and as a national community still has not even come close to recovering from the immeasurable damage that has been done to it. This

Make Ex-Prisoners Who've Paid Their Debts to Society
Full Citizens Again by Outlawing Discrimination in
Employment, Housing & Voting

is because, for over three centuries, African-Americans were openly relegated to second and third-class citizenry, largely by the employment of the exact same disenfranchising social and legal disallowances that are now mainly levied against ex-prisoners.

It is interesting to note that, during the multiple centuries of open and undisguised discrimination against African-Americans, there were very few socially discriminatory laws on the books against people for being convicted of crimes.[8] During those times, if a company or community wanted to discriminate against African-Americans or any other specific group, they could just do so explicitly and without explanation or consequence. This meant that any laws and practices that would specifically target ex-prisoners for social disenfranchisement would basically only apply to whites, since African-Americans and other non-white groups were already wholly or partly disallowed and disenfranchised. This may very well explain why there were few anti-ex-prisoner laws and practices on the books for so long in segregated

- 11 -

Make Ex-Prisoners Who've Paid Their Debts to Society
Full Citizens Again by Outlawing Discrimination in
Employment, Housing & Voting

pre-Civil War era America.

The fact that there weren't such harsh anti-ex-prisoner laws and practices at times when they would only affect whites also strongly suggests that these fairly new and standardized American ex-prisoner discriminatory practices are not colorblind, to say the least. Because previously, being a white "felon" in America was never considered that big of a deal. Case in point: Even the U.S. Presidency, an institution that until very recently has always been held by white men, has never had any specific rules that disallow a person from becoming president if that person has a felony conviction.[9] The U.S. Constitution even permits a convicted felon to be a member of Congress, even if they are still in prison.[10] Until about the mid 1970's, white convicted felons were not generally excluded from procuring high-level corporate and executive jobs and criminal convictions certainly did not prevent anyone from procuring low-level manual labor and service jobs.[11]

Make Ex-Prisoners Who've Paid Their Debts to Society
Full Citizens Again by Outlawing Discrimination in
Employment, Housing & Voting

Today, even low-wage service occupations, which
are still typically worked by non-whites to the tune of
about 80% in a country that is nearly 70% white,[12]
have specific and general policies that disallow
employment based on having a felony criminal
record.[13] Most of these anti-ex-prisoner policies are
mandatory; it is not possible to override them
subjectively or legally. While there are indeed many
whites today who are affected by ex-prisoner
discrimination, statistics clearly show that non-whites,
especially African-Americans and Latinos, are hurt
much more by it.[14] As of 2020, African-Americans are
convicted and sentenced to serve time in jail at about
five times the rate of white Americans. Among
African-American males born in 2001, one in three will
go to prison at some point during their lifetimes. One
in six Latino males will also. By contrast, one out of
every seventeen white males are expected to go to
prison. Among women, one in one hundred and
eleven white women, one in eighteen black women,
and one in forty-five Latina women will go to prison at
some point.[15] This means that the burdensome weight

Make Ex-Prisoners Who've Paid Their Debts to Society
Full Citizens Again by Outlawing Discrimination in
Employment, Housing & Voting

of the harsh and debilitating social consequences of being a person convicted of a crime in America is mainly being carried by the racial minorities of America. And it is not because they are somehow naturally more inclined to criminal activity.

Since Reconstruction, the unemployment rate for African-American and Latino men has consistently been about 50% higher than the unemployment rate of white men.[16] The incarceration and poverty rates for African-American and Latino women reflect similarly if not exactly the same when compared to white women, about 50% higher.[17] These are some of the main underlying reasons why there is and has been such a big and consistent wealth gap in America between white and non-white families. Today, the average white family possesses about ten times the wealth of the average African-American family and about eight times that of the average Latino family.[18] When it comes to facts and statistics like these and all the others we've cited, it is important to know, and really, it must be clearly understood, that none of

Make Ex-Prisoners Who've Paid Their Debts to Society
Full Citizens Again by Outlawing Discrimination in
Employment, Housing & Voting

them are a happenstance or naturally occurring issue. They happened, and are continuing to happen, by design and on purpose.

Throughout America, the rights and social abilities that individuals convicted of any felony offense lose varies state by state. But in every state as well as the federal government, ex-felons are statutorily excluded from many aspects of public and professional life. Generally, this includes restrictions on everything from housing to whom they can associate with. For the most part, ex-felons can never:

- be state or federally employed
- bear arms
- become a corporate director
- be an executor or administrator of an estate
- be a funeral director
- be a corporate officer
- be a physical therapist
- be a liquor dealer
- sit on a jury
- be a realtor
- be an engineer
- be an accountant
- be a surveyor

Make Ex-Prisoners Who've Paid Their Debts to Society
Full Citizens Again by Outlawing Discrimination in
Employment, Housing & Voting

- be a medical doctor
- be a chiropractor
- adopt children
- get government assistance or welfare
- get a student loan
- get federally funded housing
- rent an apartment
- be a security guard or bodyguard
- be a bondsman
- be a teacher

Moreover, ex-felons generally can forget about being employed within any of the following fields in any capacity: banking, medicine, psychology, psychiatry, marriage and domestic counseling, cosmetology, veterinary science, real estate, the security industry, pawn brokerage, education, pharmaceuticals, law, electrology, travel, accounting,[19] and there are dozens and dozens more. Too many to list here.

The fact is, and not just with respect to employment, the "felony" category within the American penal codes and laws is now being used as justifiable cover for ex-prisoner discrimination where it should not apply. The word "felony" used to be used to describe very serious

Make Ex-Prisoners Who've Paid Their Debts to Society
Full Citizens Again by Outlawing Discrimination in
Employment, Housing & Voting

crimes committed against society, but since the
American Prison Industrial Complex was created and
mass incarceration (of minorities) has become the
norm, its use has become expanded to the point that
many low-level and even petty crimes are now
considered felonies. Now, if a typical person gets a
felony on their record, their life immediately becomes
much harder and employment-related success
becomes nearly impossible. Getting tagged with the
"felon" label in America today basically means you
aren't a full citizen anymore and subject to legal
enslavement. As stated in the United States
Constitution, the Thirteenth Amendment, ratified in
1865: "Neither slavery nor involuntary servitude,
*except as a punishment for crime whereof the party
shall have been duly convicted,* shall exist within the
United States, or any place subject to their
jurisdiction."[20]

Predictably, as we can clearly see via incarceration
statistics since 1865 and especially over the last half-
century, this antisocial designation of "slave" or

Make Ex-Prisoners Who've Paid Their Debts to Society
Full Citizens Again by Outlawing Discrimination in
Employment, Housing & Voting

"involuntary servant" has tended to fall much more heavily on racial minorities and the poor.[21] By far, the largest groups of people who predictably become incarcerated and subsequently designated as felons for life are non-white and poor. To boot, field studies have been done that suggest that whites with criminal felony records are still not nearly as affected by ex-prisoner discrimination as non-whites. White felons tend to still be hired for jobs at rates similar or higher than blacks with no criminal record.[22] When taking all these facts, studies, and statistics into account, it goes without saying that ex-felon and ex-prisoner discrimination and disenfranchisement within the employment sector is not only counterproductive and wrong in general, but that it is also systematically applied in a purposefully more unfair and racist way.

The same thing is also being done with respect to housing and voting. Most Americans are already familiar with the fact that the employment and voting sectors discriminate against ex-prisoners and those with criminal records. Most people have or had jobs

Make Ex-Prisoners Who've Paid Their Debts to Society
Full Citizens Again by Outlawing Discrimination in
Employment, Housing & Voting

and have voted before, so they have had to become at least loosely aware of the requirements and disqualifications for both. However, it is less known how the housing sector discriminates against ex-prisoners, mainly because homeowners and renters without criminal records typically are never confronted with this reality since it doesn't affect them and isn't highly publicized. Most often, the written anti-ex-prisoner policies and requirements of for-sale or for-rent residential properties is in the fine print of the paperwork and never gets looked at or discussed once a background check has been conducted.

Conducting criminal background checks for residential stay is another much-abused vehicle of ex-prisoner discrimination. Background checks are a standard procedure today even when just trying to find somewhere to live. Just as much or even more emphasis is put on the outcome of a background check as on a prospective buyer or renter's ability to pay when considering a person for contractual residential stay. In most all apartments, townhomes,

Make Ex-Prisoners Who've Paid Their Debts to Society
Full Citizens Again by Outlawing Discrimination in
Employment, Housing & Voting

gated communities and HOAs, with few exceptions, if you cannot pass the background check, you cannot live there, not even as a temporary guest of a current resident. There are well-known cases where even ex-athlete multimillionaire ex-prisoners have been forced to live in hotels long-term because they were not being allowed to buy homes in the more secure residential areas within their cities.[23]

As for voting, most of the ancestors of the people who are now mainly being disqualified from voting by anti-ex-prisoner discriminatory laws and policies also were prohibited from voting under a different social guise—a fact which, of course, is hardly coincidental. There have always been blatant and not-so-blatant efforts made to nullify the vote of African-Americans in particular. This supposedly un-American dichotomy is, in reality, as American as apple pie. Even as this book is being written, there is a blatant and strong national effort taking place by way of the Republican Party in dozens of states to further limit the voting prowess of African-Americans after African-American

Make Ex-Prisoners Who've Paid Their Debts to Society
Full Citizens Again by Outlawing Discrimination in
Employment, Housing & Voting

and Democratic voting blocs were proven to be instrumental in removing Donald Trump from office. Just recently, Georgia became the first state to reenact Jim Crow-style laws by passing a bill that overtly seeks to limit the effectiveness of the African-American vote in the state.[24]

Keeping ex-prisoners from voting does not benefit society in any way, and to our knowledge there has yet to be a succinct argument made by anyone as to why this anti-democratic practice even exists in modern American society. Furthermore, it also presents a clear-cut scenario of mass taxation without representation, which was the very sentiment and ideal behind the American Revolution[25] and the subsequent founding of this nation. But if voting is indeed just a privilege and not a right, it seems that there really is only one reason why such an important privilege ever actually gets revoked—being convicted of a felony. It's an unnecessary and undemocratic form of bias and disenfranchisement aimed at low-hanging fruit. It's a way to legally discount and delete

Make Ex-Prisoners Who've Paid Their Debts to Society
Full Citizens Again by Outlawing Discrimination in
Employment, Housing & Voting

the influence of many Americans that other Americans feel should never have a voice in this democracy. No matter how many people irrationally support and defend ex-prisoner voting disenfranchisement, it is just plain wrong.

Like chattel slavery and legalized racism, both of which at certain points had the support of the majority of white Americans,[26] anti-ex-prisoner discrimination and disenfranchisement is untenable and *has* to end. That is, if America intends on ever actually being "the land of the free" for *all* Americans and not just for certain Americans. **Excluding citizens who have previously committed crimes and have convictions and were incarcerated—and therefore have paid their debts to society—from accessing the constituents of the American Dream is no different than excluding and discriminating based on race, religion, nationality, sexual orientation or gender.** Although world history is littered with examples of efforts to do so, there isn't and never has been any moral or logical justification for societies to essentially create low social categories

Make Ex-Prisoners Who've Paid Their Debts to Society
Full Citizens Again by Outlawing Discrimination in
Employment, Housing & Voting

of human beings by embracing policies of selective discrimination and disenfranchisement.

All discrimination is fear-based. There are various justifications that people give for discriminating against other people but they are generally always wrong, especially when blanketly applied to whole groups of people. And the resulting negative internalized feelings and effects on the lives of unfairly disenfranchised and discriminated-against groups of people are always the same: much lower communal productivity alongside rampant and long-lasting levels of hopelessness, anger, and resentment against the dominant society that allowed it. The resulting subsurface negative energy hurts the entire nation in so many ways; from creating unnecessary social tensions and problems, to more crimes being committed as a direct result of disenfranchised people leading dissatisfied lives, and to some extent, rightly blaming the larger society for it. It goes without saying that this scenario is not good for the progressiveness and overall sustainability of any nation or society.

Make Ex-Prisoners Who've Paid Their Debts to Society
Full Citizens Again by Outlawing Discrimination in
Employment, Housing & Voting

Today, Americans who are ex-prisoners, for all intents and purposes, are treated as undeclared de facto non-citizens. No American should ever be put into a non-citizen category for any reason except a legal renouncement of citizenship. Right now, America has nearly thirty million people, mostly people of color, who are effectively non-citizens due to convictions and incarceration.[27] Anti-ex-prisoner policies and laws have created a revolving door of racial discrimination, over-incarceration, generational poverty, and corporate and government monetary profit from this new-age continuance of the American Slavery Experience, now aimed at ex-prisoners. This must change. Nationally, the current and generally super-punitive and degenerative approach to aiding ex-prisoner societal reacclimatization should be replaced with policies and procedures that allow for the full citizenship rights of ex-prisoners to be restored or never taken in the first place. Nothing good, grand, or tangible is gained by society making it harder for its ex-prisoner citizens to survive. Yet, much can be gained by society removing all of the wholly

Make Ex-Prisoners Who've Paid Their Debts to Society
Full Citizens Again by Outlawing Discrimination in
Employment, Housing & Voting

unnecessary and unsmart roadblocks it places in the lives of millions of ex-prisoners, so that they have a real and genuine chance at rehabilitation and success.

Again, in the past, there were no laws that would prohibit most ex-prisoners from obtaining gainful employment or housing. It would greatly benefit American society to reinstate many of those same types of commonsense post-release policies and practices where ex-prisoners are concerned. **Discrimination and disenfranchisement of any kind against any group within the American citizenry should be permanently outlawed.** Specifically, there is no reason for discrimination and disenfranchisement against ex-prisoners other than to continue punishment for offenses committed. If a person commits a crime that society feels they can never fully pay for or is a proven continuous danger to society, then that person should never be let out of prison. However, if a person is let out of jail or prison and completes probation, parole or supervised release, that person has paid their full and proper debt to

Make Ex-Prisoners Who've Paid Their Debts to Society
Full Citizens Again by Outlawing Discrimination in
Employment, Housing & Voting

society and shouldn't be punished further. The way the system operates now, most ex-prisoners can *never* fully pay for their crime, especially if it was classified as a felony and the ex-prisoner is a person of color.

Making ex-prisoners who've paid their debts to society full citizens again by outlawing discrimination against them in employment, housing and voting is, in our opinion, one of the paramount civil rights issues of our generation. The lifetime discrimination against ex-prisoners represents the origin and epitome of a popularized American social phenomenon that is now known as "cancel culture," which is a negative form of ostracism in which people are expelled out of social and professional circles for untoward behavior or statements. Such a culture wallows in negativity and unforgiveness and does nothing to help create a better America. We believe that the purpose and duty of those who seek to create a better America is to build into the future by correcting the mistakes we've made in the past. While there obviously are those who are content to have us stay as we were in the past as a

Make Ex-Prisoners Who've Paid Their Debts to Society
Full Citizens Again by Outlawing Discrimination in
Employment, Housing & Voting

country, progression can only come with change, not stagnancy. Moreover, the realest and most long-lasting progression always comes whenever and wherever there is genuine good will towards men.

Here's something to think about: If the American mainland were ever invaded by a foreign nation, history and wartime protocol dictates that we would likely immediately release all but the very worst prisoners in expectance of them joining the fighting ranks. In the recent Russian invasion of Ukraine, Ukrainian prisoners were released to fight.[28] In our own past times of war, as in during the Civil War, both World Wars, and Vietnam, men who were accused or convicted of crimes were often given the choice to enlist in the military in lieu of trial or prison. And no one ever balked or voiced a problem with that policy.[29] Thus, there are countless veterans and heroes to whom America owes its sovereignty and very existence to who were also ex-prisoners and/or convicted felons or potentially so. This is because, despite them being felons and ex-prisoners, they were

Make Ex-Prisoners Who've Paid Their Debts to Society
Full Citizens Again by Outlawing Discrimination in
Employment, Housing & Voting

also Americans. This is why *all* Americans, even those who have been convicted of a crime and incarcerated and released, rightly deserve an interminable chance to achieve the American Dream. For ex-prisoners to have that chance, we must eliminate and outlaw all means of discrimination and disenfranchisement against them. Otherwise, the main stated ideal of America—the land of the free—will continue to be more a valiant grandiose idea than an achieved reality.

2

Refocus the Tenets of Incarceration
on Rehabilitation & Life Correction

This is the plain and simple truth that most U.S. politicians will never admit publicly: For decades, America has had an intake of millions of people into its criminal justice systems that should never have been there. At the time of the writing of this book, as has also been the case many times in the past, there are highly publicized political discussions going on about revamping criminal justice systems on the state and federal levels. These discussions always come up every so often within the political spectrum. Most of the time, they are not serious discussions about bringing about a much-needed major downsizing of these systems by way of conducting a sensible and widespread makeover of the way justice, punishment and rehabilitation are rendered in this country. In the past, whenever these types of discussions concluded, there was never any resulting action that brought about major change and a better overall situation for ex-prisoners and the American public.

For example, today, the political discussions about revamping criminal justice systems are mostly about creating more fiscal efficiency within the industry, saving taxpayer money and retaining jobs. There is talk about converting some elements of the expensive one-site, super-restrictive physical incarceration model into more lucrative state, federal and private enterprises involving virtual and multi-site less-restrictive supervised home-based incarceration for low-security prisoners. Again, these are the types of unserious, chameleonic, short-range things that are typically discussed and sometimes done whenever the subject of criminal justice reform comes up in American politics. From the perspective of those most affected and all who are right-minded, political leaders slickly not addressing and correcting the main and pressing issue (mass incarceration) in such a way for so long is directly akin to purposeful subversion. It belies a concerted interest and effort by them and their constituents to continue the status quo in one way or another.

Although there are a large number of existing government programs and policies that seemingly address the need for rehabilitation and life correctional aid for prisoners and ex-prisoners, for the most part, they have failed. Halfway houses, in-prison residential drug programs, pre-release and post-release counseling, and probationary and parole services, even if they were actually set up to truly aid ex-prisoners, which they are not, cannot offset the crippling effects of the social disenfranchisement that ex-prisoners have to deal with. **To put it plainly, if ex-prisoners are to be given a real chance at turning their lives around for the better, there must be a strong and lasting synergetic conjunction between pre-release preparation and post-release opportunities.** Just having one or the other will not suffice. Ex-prisoner post-release opportunity is just as important as prisoner pre-release preparation; one makes no sense without the other. Therefore, in conjunction with making post-release opportunities available for ex-prisoners, there needs to be a systemwide refocusing on real rehabilitation and life correction that prepares prisoners to fully take advantage of awaiting opportunities.

For quite some time, many American institutions of incarceration have been mislabeled and misnamed "correctional institutions" while others are simply referred to as prisons, jails and penitentiaries. The problem with this is that there is little to no difference between them other than the security designation of the inmates inside of them. There is no more "correction" going on inside the institutions that are labeled "correctional" than in the ones that are not. We, the authors, know this to be true by firsthand experience, a combined twenty-two-plus years of it, inside state and federal prison systems. Although the concept of two different types of incarceration is indeed viable (incarceration that heavily focuses on correction vs. incarceration that does not), the proper application of that notion has yet to materialize. The fact is, the criminal justice systems of America are too focused on rendering and ensuring punishment rather than directing their main energies into rendering and ensuring life correction skills are obtained, along with the ability for ex-prisoners to put them to use once released.

If there are to be these two distinct styles of detention for incarcerated Americans, it should be very clear as to what their differences are and there should be little to no mixing of the two. This, in our view, is key. As it stands today, the notions of correctional incarceration and punitive incarceration basically go hand in hand; the words "correctional" and "punitive" are even synonymous in American dictionaries.[30] However, in reality, there is obviously nothing correctional about being punished. Bearing the recidivism rate in mind, it's clear that punishment does very little to correct tendencies for bad behavior. There is a viable argument that it is more likely to worsen bad behavior over the long run rather than improve it. **In shaping behavior for the positive, and in addition to being more humane, reward works much**

better than punishment as a shaping tool. This is undoubtedly true, even when it comes to training and handling animals. Positive reward over punishment is one of the training hallmarks of the renowned dog trainer Cesar Millan of *Dog Whisperer* fame.[31] It is also the consistently preferred method of training for zookeepers.[32] Likewise, when it comes to influencing the behavior of corrigible human beings, there are many statistics and facts that clearly show that reward-based approaches are much more effective than the enforcement of punishment.[33]

Within the juvenile criminal justice system alone, over 1,500 institutions are labeled and characterized as being "correctional facilities,"[34] though most of them do little more than sparsely house, clothe and feed their residents. On the streets, many of these juvenile facilities have fierce and violent reputations and are known to be even worse than high-security adult penitentiaries. Correlatively, statistics show that juvenile offender recidivism rates are consistently higher than adult offender recidivism rates.[35] So, regardless of whatever attempts are made or claimed to be made at actually being correctional, as so many institutional names suggest, if those efforts to "correct" behaviors, attitudes and outlooks do not show positive results in real-world post-release scenarios, then they clearly aren't effective and thus are just semantical exercises in futility. Because it's not only about providing avenues for prisoners' rehabilitation while they are incarcerated; it's also about prisoners having hope and knowing that they will be afforded a real opportunity to start over once released. Because of how ex-prisoners are treated in American society, many people end up developing a fatalistic outlook on life after becoming incarcerated and thus do not take rehabilitative efforts seriously once they become aware of how difficult their lives will be from that point on. Which greatly increases the likelihood of them reoffending at some point.

We believe that there must be a correlating effort by society to allow for life correction efforts on the part of ex-prisoners to actually bear fruit. Ex-prisoners must be afforded the ability to put newly acquired behaviors and attitudes and outlooks to use in society.

Otherwise, just as we have been seeing for some time now, any newly acquired behaviors, attitudes and outlooks will fade and cease to exist and those potentially reformed ex-prisoners will likely relapse back into negativity and reoffend. For qualifying prisoners who want to engage in rehabilitative and life-corrective programming as opposed to just serving time, they should be placed in facilities that accommodate that. Prisoners who do not qualify or want it should be placed in regular lockup-style facilities. Institutional organization should be set up in such a way that prisoners who are serious about learning new behaviors and correcting their life's path would typically not be housed with prisoners who are not. The same way that the Army, Marines, Navy and Airforce enlistees are housed and trained separately because of the difference in knowledge and skills that are required for each branch, prisoners should be separated based on not just security levels but also on rehabilitative effort and engagement.

For violent crimes and other crimes that carry lengthy sentences, high-level rehabilitative effort through programming should be mandatory for all those convicted before they are released. Sentences should reflect that this is mandatory and the lack of completion should mean serving significantly more time in prison. If a person wants to get out of prison, then that person will undertake those rehabilitative efforts. But what is just as important is their ability to function in society without undue obstruction or discrimination once released. **We should not be releasing uncorrected or unrehabilitated criminal-minded people back into society. Likewise, we should not further punish and disenfranchise ex-prisoners who are in fact rehabilitated.** To do either or both is to ensure continuous failure, as we have already seen for some time now.

On the other hand, if what we are suggesting were to be adopted nationwide, we would certainly have more success. America undoubtedly would begin to see drastic reductions in crime, recidivism, poverty, addiction, unemployment, and nonconforming attitudes and behaviors on the part of most ex-prisoners, with measurable increases in post-release productivity. Which, according to the long-stated objectives of our criminal justice systems and politicians, are the ultimate goals.

3

Universally Ban Cash Bail

American criminal justice systems treat people better if they are rich and guilty than if they are poor and innocent, and the system of cash bail has a lot to do with that. The system of cash bail is one of the most discriminatory aspects of American criminal justice systems. It literally and openly gives preferential treatment to those who have the financial means to pay for their pre-trial/pre-conviction release from jail. Statistics have long shown that there are numerous advantages to being out on bail vs. being locked up when litigating a criminal case. Statistics have also shown that, by far, the flaws of the cash bail system disproportionately affect African-Americans and Latinos, who generally have much lower net worths, fewer assets and less access to cash than whites.[36] This results in county and city jails continuously teeming with mainly minority defendants who otherwise would be released on bond sans their lack of access to money.

The purpose of a bond is to ensure your physical presence at future court proceedings and to activate your constitutional right to a presumption of innocence until you are proven guilty in a court of law by a jury or judge.[37] That very sacred presumption of innocence is the only thing that would afford a person the ability to protect, maintain and continue many important aspects of their pre-arrest life that would otherwise create undue duress on them and their loved ones if they were in jail. That is the very reason why it was important enough to be put into the U.S. Constitution—to protect the livelihood of an accused person up until that person was proven to actually be guilty of a crime.

The price that people pay for not being able to make bond is tremendous and life-altering. In a nation where citizens are supposed to be innocent until proven guilty, the reality is that it is the other way around for poor people; they are effectively guilty until proven innocent. And even when actually proven innocent after spending months or years in jail, they are not compensated for the losses that were incurred due to their lengthy and frivolous pre-conviction incarceration. Jobs are lost, families suffer and are broken, precious time is wasted and spent in a horrible environment, yet they are typically not even offered an apology. Again, it is basically only the poor that are subjected to this "guilty until proven innocent" mistreatment by our judicial systems. The system of cash bail criminalizes poverty and does little to nothing to benefit or protect society in the process, as the overwhelming majority of people who are affected by the cash bail system do not pose a threat to public safety.[38]

Arrestees that are given "no bond" statuses are totally deprived of the presumption of innocence. There is an argument to be made that all criminally accused citizens should be afforded a presumption of innocence and either given a makeable bond or released on their own recognizance. However, in certain cases, especially those involving violent or serious crimes with very high levels of proof of guilt and high likelihood of repeat behavior or flight risk, it is understandable and proper to not offer bonds. The seriousness of the crime and a preponderance of evidence have to be considered in the bond-making process. But for the most part, own-recognizance bonds, supervised or not, should be given to accused citizens who have not been proven guilty via the judicial process. Doing that ensures a certain level of fairness and mitigates unnecessary risks that come into play when innocent people are incarcerated pre-conviction. These risks include an elevated potential for suicide[39] and the potential for them to plead guilty in exchange for being sentenced to the time they've already served. The fact is, many people do the latter just so they can get out and get back to work and back to their families. This is very common but negatively consequential in the long term for those that do it.[40]

Between 1970 and 2015, the increase in the use of pretrial detention shot up more than 433%,[41] which coincides with the rise of mass incarceration as a general tool of American social policy. As a result, on any given day, there are close to half a million *innocent* people sitting in jail because they cannot make bond.[42] Every day, there are tens of millions of dollars being spent by federal and state governments to house, feed and maintain innocent people who shouldn't be in jail.[43] Private-owned prisons reap profits from the temporary incarceration of these innocent people. A very important factor within the nature of these statistical numbers is the heavy lobbying power of the multi-billion-dollar per year for-profit bail industry that has been allowed to run amuck over the last several decades.[44] Capitalism has infiltrated and taken over our criminal justice systems on every level; from the supposed administration of justice in the courtrooms, to the dispensing of punishment and supposed rehabilitation in the jail cells and dorms. If nothing else, the administering of justice should be two things: blind to bias and not-for-sale. America's criminal justice systems are neither blind to bias nor not-for-sale, and the cash bail system is part of the reason why this is true.

There are a few states that are currently reforming their cash bail systems, but as of the writing of this book Illinois is the only state that has effectively eliminated it.[45] As Illinois has recognized, there are viable alternatives to cash bail that are just as effective at ensuring the presence of the accused in court for proceedings, like non-surety bonds. The only reason to have a cash bail system is to create income for local, state and federal budgets. Again, capitalist for-profit principles have little to no place in the process of administering justice, as this negates the very idea of justice and fairness and the presumption of innocence. **The administering of justice, real justice, requires the continuous ratification of fairness at all costs by its administrators.** In the case of the cash bail system, it is indisputably clear, and has been for a long time now, that it is a fundamentally unfair and biased process that duly discriminates against minorities and the poor. Therefore, we must continue to work toward and demand an end to the usage of cash bail in the United States of America.

4

Ban Private Prisons

As this book was being written, the newly elected president, Joe Biden, within the first two weeks of his inauguration, is signing an executive order that, pursuant to his campaign promises to the African-American community, purports to ban the usage of private prisons by the federal government.[46] The problem with this is, it does not ban anything for real. Citing a need to "reduce profit-based incentives to incarcerate," the order will prevent the Department of Justice from pursuing new contracts with private prisons during his administration. However, it won't put an immediate halt to contracts that are already in use, which are plentiful and substantial. Essentially, he is leaving the private prison industry intact so that it can resume full normal operations under a different administration in the future. Additionally, Biden's executive order has no jurisdiction over the use of private prisons by states, which are the main users of private prisons that do not operate under the Department of Justice, as it is a federal agency. In other words, just more double talk and more broken promises and unserious political dialogue not meant to spurn real and lasting change. As stated in Chapter 2, this is what our politicians always do when it comes to these issues.

Joe Biden made a pre-election statement that "the federal government should not use private facilities for any detention, including the detention of undocumented immigrants."[47] It rings hollow when you consider the fact that, almost two years into his administration, nearly 80% of the people detained by Homeland Security and Immigration Enforcement were still being housed and/or managed by privately owned detention centers.[48] Given Biden's history and central role in legislating the horrendous 1994 Crime Bill, which disproportionately impacted communities of color through the implementation of policies such as the "three strikes, you're out" rule and the expansion of the death penalty, it's not entirely a surprise that he pulled a bait and switch once he was elected.[49] Though he has publicly stated that he has changed course on criminal justice and now wants to see large-scale reform, including banning private prisons and jails and lowering the recidivism rate,[50] he has done little to nothing to date to actually bring that into fruition in a meaningful way.

The obvious truth seems to be that Biden never really intended to follow through with his stated goal of banning private prisons. He is now slickly alluding to limitations to his powers[51] that he never discussed or disclosed before he took office. Again, this is par for the course and doesn't break precedent with his presidential predecessors and colleagues on both sides of the political party isle. However, the big problem with the continuance of this bad policy of allowing private prisons is that, aside from the fact that it is an immoral remnant of plantation slavery that's based on corporate greed, racism, and rogue capitalism, it also pretty much guarantees that high levels of crime, incarceration, and recidivism will continue to plague American society well into the foreseeable future. Because crime has been made into an industry to be profited from by investors, more investment and lobbying money has poured into the industry. So much so, that it now fully controls the rulemaking and regulation of the industry through the politicians, just like most other large privately owned industries in America.

American politics, politicians, and lawmaking in general are all about capital investment and lobbying, and that is one of the natural flaws of our democracy. But certain social services provided by the state shouldn't be included in this. Some social services and government industries should exist apart and separate from those tenets of capitalism that only exist for the purpose of creating and maximizing profit. The criminal justice system is one of them. Otherwise, there will be (and currently is) a widespread unspoken motivation on the part of many to keep the courts, jails, and prisons as full as possible. This then leads to the creation and enforcement of biased and unjust laws and policies by politicians, court systems and law enforcement. The tradeoff of high corporate profits in exchange for guaranteed high crime and incarceration rates is not the act of a smart and just society that values its citizenry and wants to create a better future for all.

A segment of American wealth and industry being built on people privately owning prisons, which are basically ran as profit engines and punitive human labor and storage facilities, is indeed the modern-day evolution and continuation of the American wealth and industry that was built on a system of owning slaves. Only with this schematic, it is carried out under the general and former expectation of prisons and jails being entities that only exist to serve the just needs and interests of the public, not a system of slavery or servitude unjustly based on race and profit. But the fact that profitmaking has been allowed to be so heavily involved in the process of administering criminal justice further negates even the semblance of a fair and impartial system. People having confidence in the fairness and impartiality of the system should be an absolute necessity. The allowance of mostly minority-filled privately owned prisons in today's supposedly progressive America, among many other things, has further eroded that confidence to an all-time low.

The bottom line is, there is no good reason to have a private prison industry in America. It's a fairly new phenomena that began in 1983[52] that needs to be discontinued as soon as possible if America is serious about becoming something decidedly better than it has been in the past, particularly when it comes to its treatment of minorities. Joe Biden made that promise to end private prisons to the African-American community for a reason; they are disproportionately affected. His 2020 criminal justice platform articulated, "To build safe and healthy communities, we need to rethink who we're sending to jail, how we treat those in jail, and how we help them get the health care, education, jobs, and housing they need to successfully rejoin society after they serve their time."[53] Barack Obama and even Donald Trump have voiced similar sentiments when speaking on the subject of criminal justice reform. The problem with this is, when you actually look at the totality of the criminal justice system—the laws, procedures, and court behavior; the recidivism rates; incarceration rates; the racial makeup of America's prisons and revolving door jail populations—you can clearly see that not much is changing in the right direction, despite all the good-sounding talk. Thus, the private prison industry is currently poised to become a multi-generational destructive industry in the United States of America.

Prison ownership is essentially prisoner ownership. Thus, privately owned prisons are little more than simulated continuations of for-profit plantation servitude with a better excuse for existing. Ending private prisons should be a top priority for Americans who value the rule of law and believe that fairness and equality should reign supreme over profit motive when it comes to administering and ensuring justice.

5

Require Prisoners to Submit Feasible Life Action Plans Before Release and Enable Halfway Houses, Probation, Parole & Supervised Release Offices to Make Resources Available to Support Those Plans

Post-release programs are important and necessary tools in aiding ex-prisoners' proper reintroduction into society. Parole, probation, supervised release and halfway houses are the main four post-release systems and programs available and recoursed by most ex-prisoners. These programs exist partly to protect the public, but they are also supposed to be positive and helpful buffers between being incarcerated and being free. For a person who has spent significant time inside jail or prison and away from normal society, trying to reacclimate oneself to living and engaging normally within society is often a very daunting task. When you throw in all the legal discrimination and disadvantages that ex-prisoners face in society, it can seem nearly impossible to do, even with the assistance of post-release programs.

The big problem with all of these programs is that they are not mainly directed toward fully supporting the reacclimation of ex-prisoners in society, despite being in the position to offer the most meaningful assistance. They are all, in fact, far more punitive and negatively assumptive in nature than supportive. Their overall approach is basically being a seamless continuation of the overly punitive penal system. Which is the polar opposite of what they should be if effectively lowering American crime, recidivism, and incarceration rates are the ultimate goals.

What is sorely lacking is a sense of compassion. The same sense of compassion that is warranted and given to other citizens who happen to not have been caught committing a crime. To be clear, every adult has broken the law before; whether it was speeding in a car or not paying every cent owed in taxes or illegal drug use or something else. Statistics say that basically 100% of American adults have broken the law in their lives at one time or another.[54] But for some reason, those citizens who have been caught committing a crime are not entitled to the same compassion and treatment as everyone else, no matter their desperation. Put simply, this is just plain wrong. In every meaningful way, this is wrong and certainly isn't the smartest way for us to go about formulating and administering effective post-release programming. And the most obvious, clear-cut way to tell whether or not it is effective is to look at the recidivism numbers.

Specifically, the compassion we are speaking of is making *meaningful* resources and assistance available to ex-prisoners who need them. Since the Great Depression, America has always had a welfare system that offers meaningful assistance and resources to citizens that temporarily fall between the economic cracks of society.[55] However, not only are ex-prisoners generally prohibited from eligibility for welfare benefits, there are no real programs that offer that level of assistance to ex-prisoners, despite them being the most in need of temporary economic assistance in most cases. Once again, this discrimination is justified with the pervasive and unreasonable notion that anyone who has ever been to jail or prison should generally be assumed to be bad and of less value, for life. Thus, in lieu of being given real assistance or a helping hand, those "bad" people should only be given a hard way to go. America basically never forgives you if you are ever caught committing a crime, especially a felony, and the general idea of never forgiving is deeply encapsulated within all parts of American society, post-release programs included.

If we are to drastically reduce future crime and incarceration rates, we must begin to do things very differently with regards to post-release programs. In addition to some of the things they do now, they should be government equipped and funded to be able to provide more meaningful assistance. Such things as interactive counseling and consultation with successful ex-prisoners, livable wage labor-finding assistance, and direct temporary financial assistance. None of them should be for-profit (halfway houses). If these things were put into policy and practice, we believe that all prisoners should then be required to submit feasible life action plans that fit their individual circumstances before being placed in a post-release program and given access to those resources. With such a format, post-release programs would be an effective synergetic continuance and connecting outlet for the specific training and preparation that was received before release from jail or prison (as described in Chapter 2). This would be putting resources where they are truly needed and can do the most good for the overall health and wellbeing of our society. The return on this type of long-term investment is very likely to be better and more positive than the return we've been getting from the short-term, overly punitive policies and practices we have now.

When it comes to the formulation and activation of criminal justice policy, spending taxpayer money in a manner whereby it will do the most good should always be considered smart fiscal policy and not labeled wasteful or "soft-on-crime" whenever real and meaningful assistance for ex-prisoners is warranted. That's what has always been done in the past up to the present, to our collective detriment. Again, American ex-prisoners are taxpaying citizens too, and it is just as good for society when they are allowed to succeed as it is for all other citizens.

As a general rule, the effectiveness of all policies and practices should always be a top consideration in an advanced and progressive society. There should be a continuous, upward trend towards "getting it right" and achieving worthwhile goals and reaching stated progressive milestones. That being said, there is absolutely no question that the general approach of the post-release programs of today is not helping to curb crime, incarceration rates, or recidivism,[56] which is their main collective purpose and reason for existing. Thus, it's really a no-brainer that a smarter approach is warranted, and we have every reason to believe that

an approach similar to the one outlined in this chapter
represents the best and fastest way to get these
things done.

6

Make Second Offense Violent Gun or Knife Crime Carry a Mandatory Federal Life Sentence & Apply Gun Ownership Disenfranchisement to Violent Offenders Only

An interesting rumor, which many people say is factual, is that in some parts of the country during the 1800's and early 1900's, a white person who was getting out of jail after a long stay was issued a rifle, a horse, and a piece of gold.[57] The rifle was supposedly for hunting and self-protection, the horse was for transportation, and the gold was to pay for clothing and temporary shelter. However, others say that they were only issued back the gun that they had in their possession when they were arrested. Either of these could have been the case, because what is known for sure is that ex-prisoners per se, in the past, were not prohibited from owning guns. By contrast, today, if you are convicted of a crime and have to serve time, you'll likely be given less than a few hundred dollars upon release and you are prohibited from gun ownership or gun possession, for life. Today, even teenage first-time offenders who have been convicted of nonviolent felony offenses are prohibited from owning or possessing a firearm, for life.[58] This has been the law since 1968. Previously, since 1934, only violent ex-prisoners were disallowed from owning and possessing guns. Before 1934, there were no federal restrictions whatsoever on ex-prisoners owning or possessing guns.[59]

In America, unlike many other nations, firearm ownership is widespread and pervasive, partly because it is considered a right by most citizens and not a privilege.[60] The ability and right of American citizens to protect themselves with arms is guaranteed by the U.S. Constitution, hence the wording of the Second Amendment, stating "the right of the people to keep and bear Arms shall not be infringed."[61] To be clear, a right is something that is God-given, while a privilege is something that is man-given. In 2008, the Supreme Court upheld that the "Second Amendment protects an individual right to possess a firearm unconnected with service in a militia, and to use that arm for traditionally lawful purposes, such as self-defense within the home."[62] However, states and the federal government have successfully conspired to whittle down the right to bear arms and effectively redefine it as a government-given privilege that can be arbitrarily taken away for nonviolent offenses that have nothing to do with guns or violence.

In America, the only nation on earth that is known as "the land of the free," a right, or even a privilege, should not be revoked without just cause or for reasons that are not directly related to that specific revoked right or privilege. **If a person has never committed an act of violence, there is no justifiable reason to permanently prevent that person from having the ability to sufficiently protect themselves and their family with a firearm.** Just because a person has stolen or possessed drugs before, that doesn't mean that same person is more likely to commit murder or rape or assault in the future. Just because a misguided 18-year-old made a dumb decision to sell some drugs or commit some other senseless act of nonviolence, that doesn't indicate that he or she will also rob or assault someone. But society and the justice systems treat all ex-prisoners like this is the case. These types of anti-ex-prisoner suppositions really are a continuum of that same preposterous notion that all "criminals" or ex-prisoners are the same and can never be reformed and thus should never be forgiven. But we all know that this is not true.

Again, every law or policy should be based upon sound reasoning and necessity, not unproven or unwarranted fear or anything else. For nonviolent ex-prisoners to not be able to legally defend themselves, even while in their own home as specified by the 2008 Supreme Court clarification, is not only unfair and unwarranted, it exposes them, along with their families, to disproportionate and undue risk. Risk that is based upon a false and assumptive prediction of them somehow having a higher potential to commit future violence just because they are ex-prisoners. The sad fact is that it is dangerous to be unarmed in America, especially in today's times, where violent crime by violent criminals is rampant and gun ownership and gun carrying are at an all-time high. There are over a million home invasions per year in America.[63] We are living during a time when everyone has access to guns and every other person that you see is probably carrying a gun. Over 40% of American households are documented gun owners,[64] and we suspect that number is much higher in reality. Most states are adopting Stand Your Ground laws along with the recently popularized notion of Constitutional Carry,[65] which is the constitution-based right to carry a gun in public without a license or permit. In a society such as this, being permanently disarmed, especially while in the home, can and does become a death sentence for ex-prisoners and their families under certain circumstances. There are many documented incidents that showcase this dangerous and very real potentiality.[66]

The fact that a six-year-old child can legally own a firearm in most states but a nonviolent ex-prisoner cannot even reside with someone who owns a gun for fear it'll be used to commit a crime is absolutely ridiculous.[67] To boot, most of the worst mass shootings and domestic violence cases involving guns that have happened over the past twenty years were carried out by people who didn't have any criminal record at all.[68] Studies and statistics have always suggested that someone who has never been convicted of a crime is just as likely to commit an act of violence with a gun as a person who has a criminal record.[69] After all, even the very worst criminals, at some point in their lives, had no criminal record. Despite all these things being true, we know that American lawmakers would never entertain the question of preemptively disallowing all citizens the right to bear arms based on these statistics. And they shouldn't, but by that same logic, permanent gun ownership disenfranchisement should be reserved as a sanction for those citizens who have proven themselves to be a violent threat in our society.

On the flip side of the subject, in our humble but informed opinion, there should be little to no tolerance for violent crime in American society. We believe violent crime should carry the highest, most severe penalties of all crime on the federal level and that those who repeatedly commit acts of violence should be housed separately from nonviolent offenders. We believe that these two measures by themselves, though cliché and simple, would greatly help curtail America's seemingly intractable problem with violent crime. Currently, violent prisoners are typically housed with nonviolent prisoners in the federal prison system and within most of the state prison systems. This is such a tremendous problem because it greatly increases the likelihood that many nonviolent prisoners will develop violent tendencies as a means of in-prison survival. The separation of the nonviolent from the violent curtails the development of violent energy and practices in nonviolent offenders that will one day be released back into society. Additionally, the federal distinguishment, streamlining and standardizing of harsh punishment for violent crime involving deadly weapons would quickly get the word out that these types of crimes will not be tolerated. It would show that the federal government is sparing no expense to ensure each incident of violent crime committed in society is properly and uniformly addressed. As it stands, most violent crime falls within the purview and jurisdiction of the various states, which denotes the wide array of punishments, consequences, and outcomes that are typical for those who have committed violent crimes.

There are several nations and societies that currently experience the enjoyment of having virtually no violent crime, and we can learn a few things from them. The common denominators for these low-violence places are four-fold: limited access to guns; effective networks of social welfare programs; little to no tolerance for violence or the glorification of violence; and overall low crime rates. There are other indicators for low-violence societies, like the lack of international conflicts and the lack of militarization.[70] America will likely never entertain several of these characteristics, like limiting all access to firearms, demilitarization or staying out of international conflicts. Therefore, we should definitely be putting heavier efforts toward improving our social welfare programs, decreasing our overall crime rates, and removing our extremely high tolerance for violence. A good way to help with the latter two of those three things would be to make second offense violent gun or knife crime carry a mandatory federal life sentence or an otherwise lengthy term of federal incarceration. With prisons and jails being designated to house violent prisoners separately from nonviolent prisoners.

For so long, violence has been acceptingly referred to as just being part of "prison culture." New prisoners are simply told, by prison staff and other prisoners, that that's just the way it is in prison and to adjust to it and shut up. But what we know about this culture is, it shouldn't be accepted and doesn't have to exist—it has been *allowed* to exist. Encouraged, even, for a very long time within American penal systems. Why, you might ask? Well, we can say that it is a result of

negligence or a result of bad longstanding policies.
We can say whatever we want or make whatever
excuse, but we've knowingly allowed it to happen for
a very long time. At the end of the day, the fact is, if
we're really serious about reducing violent crime in
American society, then, at the bare minimum, our
prisons should be set up to do the exact opposite of
this. That is, generally, our prisons should be set up to
strongly *discourage* and *decrease* the likelihood of the
development of violent tendencies by prisoners,
especially those convicted of nonviolent offenses who
will one day be released back into society. This can
largely be accomplished by providing total in-prison
separation between the violent and the nonviolent.

— — —

If we do the few things that are suggested in this
chapter, we believe that we can begin to see a
turnaround actually occur in real time and certainly
with respect to future generations. Violent crime has
no place in a truly civilized society. But if we cannot be
wholly civilized as human beings, we can at least try to
be as fair and as smart as we can be about how we

deal with things. We can admit and correct our mistakes. The ways that we have been dealing with violent crime haven't been the smartest and, again, the results clearly show that. Our national tolerance for violence needs to be lowered, by a lot. To do that requires the right social recipe for change. A recipe that does not include the unfair selective and totally unnecessary disenfranchisement of gun and self-defense rights of nonviolent citizens.

Across-the-board permanent gun ownership disenfranchisement for ex-prisoners or those designated to be "felons" is just one of the many discriminatory anti-ex-prisoner practices that should not exist. Many attorneys and judges, even staunch conservative "law and order" Trump-appointed Supreme Court Justice Amy Coney Barrett, agree with this, as she has argued on numerous occasions that nonviolent felons still have their Second Amendment rights.[71] In addition to all of the reasons already described, this practice also leads to racial disparities and discrimination against African-American males, who are more heavily affected by these laws and yet are simultaneously among the most in need of personal protection. Because of ex-prisoner gun ownership disenfranchisement, about one in three African-American men cannot ever legally own a gun,[72] whilst living in a society where nearly everyone else is armed and they are disproportionate victims of gun violence[73] that comes from a wide variety of communal or intercommunal directions. This means that, out of approximately twelve million adult African-American males,[74] about four million, most of whom were convicted of nonviolent offenses,[75] can never legally own or possess a firearm again. This needs to change. At the very minimum, nonviolent ex-prisoners should be allowed to keep a firearm inside of their homes or residences, for the safety and protection of themselves and their families.

7

Standardize Conjugal Visitation for Nonviolent Prisoners

Conjugal visitation is the sparingly used practice of allowing qualifying incarcerated citizens to have private unsupervised time with spouses, and on rare occasions, other family members. Though previously legal in more than seventeen states,[76] it is currently only legal in six states: New York, Washington, New Mexico, California, Mississippi, and Connecticut.[77] (America's increasingly punitive views toward prisoner treatment led to most of the other states ending the practice.) However, there are dozens of other countries that allow conjugal visitation for their prisoners.[78] The standard argument against prisoners having conjugal visits is that serving time in prison or jail should be all about punishment and thus such a thing should not be allowed. The opposing argument is usually that granting conjugal visitation to prisoners increases family bonds, helps temper prisoner stress, and is a highly effective prisoner behavioral control mechanism for prison administrators.

Typically, where it's allowed, the privilege of receiving conjugal visitation is only given to low or medium-security, compliant prisoners. Compliant, meaning having little to no *in-prison* disciplinary issues or violence. In other words, unless the prisoner has been convicted of an especially heinous offense, the nature of the offense that originally sent the prisoner to prison does not necessarily prohibit their eligibility for conjugal visitation.[79] Therefore, in most places where conjugal visits are allowed, some violent offenders get the privilege, as long as the violence they committed was not done inside of prison while serving time on their current sentence and their security level has been classified as low or medium.

Based on extensive research and factfinding on the subject of conjugal visitation for prisoners, we believe that this extracurricular practice potentially has more merits than are typically recognized, if practiced with certain additions and parameters added. First, we think that the concept of conjugal visitation should be redefined or expanded to always include offspring and other important family members, not just spouses. In other words, extended private non-conjugal visitation. Because, for many prisoners, their most important relationship may not be with a spouse; it may be with a parent, a sibling, their offspring, or a combination of any of those. On a case-by-case basis, approval for such unsupervised extended visitation should be based upon a determination of what's needed coupled with what or who is available in the life of the prisoner in question. Private time for physical and sexual connectivity is important for married couples, but private time for non-sexual physical connectivity with others who are also preeminent within the lives of ex-prisoners is just as important.

Secondly, the usage of conjugal and non-conjugal private visitation should be standardized. Contrary to what the adversaries of the more humane treatment of prisoners and ex-prisoners say, there actually isn't much downside to expanding the use of conjugal and family private visitation for prisoners. It's not only more humane, it does help keep families together, which in the long run is better and cheaper for society. **Humane treatment promotes humane behavior, the same way that inhumane mistreatment promotes inhumane misbehavior.** Thus, when it comes to "correctional" institutions, punishment, when appropriate, should not be too long-lasting and the subsequent treatment and engagement with the punished shouldn't be overly punitive. That is, if internalized respect for the process and consistent proper behavior are the desired long-term end results.

What many of these anti-prisoner advocates seem not to get or understand is, more and harsher punishment doesn't necessarily create the likelihood of future proper behavior. Not with human beings, not even with animals. Actually, it is just as likely to create resentment, hatred, hopelessness, and needless marginalization. Every wild animal that was ever made tame was done so with the utilization of a mix of generally humane treatment and temporary targeted punishment for episodes of bad behavior. The polar opposite of desired results tends to happen more often than not when this style of approach is not undertaken. This, again, goes toward explaining our consistently high recidivism rate.

We know that one of the most significant difficulties and worries that prisoners face is their families falling apart while they are serving their time. Therefore, it is very important to try to prevent such things from occurring. From society's perspective, it's understood that, without a safety net when they get out, they'll likely be back in prison. That being said, a case study of New York state prisoners in the 1980's revealed that prisoners reoffended 67% less if they had conjugal visits.[80] This is because conjugal visits not only help maintain familial ties, but also improves their overall mental health and gives them something to look forward to and (correctly) live for while serving their time. Allowing prisoners to spend quality time with their spouses almost certainly prevents divorces and family breakups. Spending quality time together is especially critical for families with children. The benefits of such visits don't only apply to the prisoner, as studies show that conjugal visitation also improves the lives of those who visit, including children.[81]

Standardizing conjugal visitation for spouses and expanding the private visitation of other important family members will provide corrigible prisoners with much-needed support and help keep them on the right track. It's clear that, if allowed to maintain close family ties through regular high-quality visitation and time-spending, families of prisoners stand a much better chance of having a healthy family life once the prison term is over. Which means less crime in society and less recidivism, which are always the twin goals of smart criminal justice policy. Within this context, as a society, we should be willing to trade this privilege for the social profit of having less crime and recidivism and stronger family units. Keeping American families together is very important, even those of prisoners and ex-prisoners. All indications point to this as being a smart move that can help turn things around with respect to our failing justice systems.

Sans those who have repeatedly committed heinous crimes and crimes of violence, regular conjugal and non-conjugal private visitation for prisoners and their families should be considered for implementation as standard national policy within America's federal and state prison systems.

8

Pay More for Industrial Prison Labor

As discussed in Chapter 4, the allowance of private-owned prisons in America bears stark but modernized resemblance, both in theme and practicality, to past-era American plantation slavery. Free and ultra-cheap forced prison labor for private gain is particularly resemblant and pervasive and bears close kinship to what was the core purpose of slavery. These stark resemblances exist because slavery was never really abolished, only renamed, redesigned and relegated only to affect incarcerated citizens. Again, it all begins with the forementioned loopholing slavery-continuing words of the Thirteenth Amendment of the U.S. Constitution, which is officially and falsely noted as the law that abolished American slavery in 1865. The Virginia Supreme Court later agreed that prisoners were "slaves of the state" in 1871.[82] So, if you become incarcerated in America, you indeed become a slave, both by definition and by law. To say that slavery ever ended in America is materially false, as it continues unimpeded to this day inside of prisons all across the country. American slavery was and is about profiting from organized free and cheap labor, with little to no rights or fair treatment for the enslaved workers. This precisely describes what is happening with regards to prison labor in America today.

Though the concept of prison labor as punishment is almost as old as the concept of prison itself, industrial prison labor is something altogether different. Since the beginning of American history, initially as a replacement for torture and mutilation, prison labor has existed and the goal and sole purpose of it was punishment.[83] Throughout American history, prisoners have typically done labor that helped prisons run better along with things that served the local communities but had nominal value in terms of financial profit for government or private entities. Sometimes they even did hard labor that served no other purpose other than punishment. Today, those types of prison labor still exist, but now a significant amount of prison labor is *not* designed for punishment or public service; it's designed for corporate profit. As a result, a large percentage of all prison workers are now performing industrial labor solely for the purpose of providing a financial benefit for corporations and all levels of government.

Industrial prison labor had its beginnings in the South right after the Civil War ended overt race-based slavery, with what was called convict leasing.[84] In the earlier forms of the practice, convict leasing provided free or very low-cost prisoner labor to private parties, such as plantation owners and corporations. Needless to say, it was a program purposefully designed to mainly target the newly freed African-American male demographic.[85] In places like Parchment Prison Farm, now Mississippi State Penitentiary, infamous for its horrendous living conditions and inhumane treatment of prisoners from 1901 to this very day,[86] convict leasing seemed to seamlessly replace plantation-based slavery. The critically acclaimed movie "Life," starring Eddie Murphy, Martin Lawrence, and Bernie Mac, showcased a true depiction of what happened to many African-American men post-Civil War up to the present day.[87] Petty charges and dubious accusations were routinely trumped up to be more serious than they were and then used to put African-American men on the "chain gang" in order to extract free labor for a period of time as well as to reinforce white supremacy.[88] From the simple vagrancy and loitering laws in the mid-late 1800's to the Crack vs. Powder and War on Drugs laws of recent times, all kinds of "legal" ruses and pretexts have been used to feed and excuse the over-policing and mass incarceration of some of the most vulnerable members of our citizenry and then allow corporations and government to utilize their ill-gotten prison labor for profit.

This is wrong on so many levels and for so many reasons, and either the practice of industrializing prison labor needs to stop altogether or prisoners should be paid significantly more for their labor than they are being paid. It begins with the federal government and the federal prison system, as they are the standard bearers for state governments and state prison systems. For example, in the federal prison system, over 17,000 prisoners work for UNICOR, which is a wholly owned Government corporation that was established by Congress in 1934.[89] Its supposed mission is to "protect society and reduce crime by preparing inmates for successful reentry through job training." UNICOR claims that its primary purpose is "not about business, but rather inmate release preparation....UNICOR assists offenders with acquiring marketable job skills so that they can one day become law-abiding, contributing members of society. The production of items and provision of services are merely by-products of those efforts."[90]

UNICOR also claims that "UNICOR is first and foremost a correctional program. UNICOR programs help reduce recidivism, reduces the amount of government spending, and compensates society. The Inmate Financial Responsibility Program (IFRP) ensures that inmates who have financial obligations contribute 50% of their earnings. That money is used to pay for court-ordered fines, victim restitution, child support, incarceration fees, and other monetary judgments. Inmates receive approximately $0.04 of each $1.00 in sales revenue, which is primarily used to repay important financial obligations."[91] Thus, despite already earning a maximum of one-sixth of the archaic and rarely used federal minimum wage, federal inmate workers with "financial obligations" must contribute half of their meager earnings to cover those expenses. Not to mention having to pay extremely high prices for prison commissary and phone calls, etc.[92] This literally means that most of them will work eight hours a day, five or six days a week for years and still get out with nothing to show for it.

Yet, UNICOR typically generates about a half billion dollars in annual sales income.[93] The products of UNICOR prison labor can be found in almost all government office buildings nationwide, as well as in everything from Microsoft computers and Boeing airplanes to Victoria's Secret lingerie and Idaho potatoes.[94] State prison industrial factories operate very similarly to UNICOR, producing large varieties of products for state-owned and privately owned corporations through something called The Prison Industry Enhancement Certification Program (PIECP).[95] In both state and federal prisons, the average industrial prison worker earns between $0.23 and $1.15 per hour doing jobs that would otherwise pay non-incarcerated citizens anywhere from ten to one hundred times more.[96]

To boot, these same workers are typically not eligible to work for a similar corporation doing similar work once they are released. The same government and private entities that proclaim to be "preparing inmates for successful reentry through job training" and that they "assist offenders with acquiring marketable job skills so that they can one day become law-abiding, contributing members of society" are the same entities that regularly support and pass laws to keep prisoners from obtaining legal employment with their acquired skills once released. How ironic is that? Is this not the very definition of sinister hypocrisy? Do not these starkly conflicting actions and statements by these entities show that their real desire and intent is to sustain and justify prison slave labor for profit? And *not* assist prisoners and ex-prisoners in becoming "law-abiding, contributing members of society" nor "protect society and reduce crime by preparing inmates for successful reentry through job training"? If they were truly interested in doing these things, they would be doing the exact opposite of what they've been doing. They would pay prisoners more for their labor and lobby to eliminate post-incarceration prisoner discrimination in the work force.

America's criminal justice systems via prisons should begin to pay more for industrial labor and maybe even incorporate mandates that require prisoners to save a large percentage of their pay for usage after release. As opposed to paying pennies on the dollar and tacking extraneous court-ordered fines, fees and restitution onto prisoners and then using their labor to collect it, making even more of their labor virtually free. If done in widespread fashion, something like this would greatly offset post-release expenses for governments and prisoners' families by redirecting resources that are currently being used punitively toward a system that pays fair labor wages to prisoners. All while promoting and encouraging the principles of hard work, frugality and self-governance. As a result, these principles would subconsciously be ingested into the psyches of corrigible prisoners as viable alternatives to criminal mindedness and criminal activity, which is exactly what we want when it comes to correctional rehabilitative programming. Not to mention that this would greatly boost the self-esteem of many prisoners, most of whom are poor, giving them a much-needed perception of hope for the future and a genuine opportunity to do things differently in their lives.

Prison labor profits, if any, should benefit the greater public and prisoners and their families, not privately owned corporations. Making prisoners work for free doing things that serve their communities is fine, but making prisoners work to make governments and multimillionaires and billionaires richer is *not* fine. That is neo-indentured servitude, which is indeed a form of slavery. Corporate involvement in prison labor and other aspects of criminal justice, as spoken about in previous chapters, is the problem. Corporations only care about their bottom line: making money. Corporations care nothing about morality, especially when it isn't being enforced by law. Therefore, if less crime and recidivism, smaller prison systems, and instilling hope for the future are truly the goals of criminal justice policy creators and administrators, like they love to tout whenever it's convenient and fits their narratives, then corporations should have no place in dictating policies or excising profit within criminal justice systems and certain aspects of law enforcement.

9

Utilize More Creative Alternatives to Incarceration for Nonviolent First-Time Offenders & Juveniles

Incarceration and probationary supervision are the two most typical forms of punishment for acts of illegality, not only in America, but in the world.[97] Probationary supervision is usually given either on the backend of a period of incarceration or as a straightaway alternative to incarceration for certain low-level or first-time offenses, both violent and nonviolent. On any given day in America within the past three decades, there were nearly two and a half million people behind bars and five million more on probation, parole or supervised release.[98] Although there are typically double the amount of people under probationary supervision than are incarcerated, the levels of incarceration for nonviolent first-time offenders, including juveniles, are still much too high.

In our view, incarceration should be considered a last resort when it comes to first-time nonviolent offenders. We believe that jail and prison sentences should primarily be reserved for violent offenders, repeat offenders and for certain high-level nonviolent offenses otherwise deemed serious enough to warrant incarceration. In other words, we think there should be a higher bar for incarcerating nonviolent American citizens, not a lower one. On the flip side, in our view, there should be no probation-only sentences handed out for violent offenses, not even first-time offenses. With rare exceptions made in some cases involving juveniles. It is violent crime and repeat offenses that generally should be targeted for deterrence through incarceration. This is because repeat offending indicates the need for harsher consequences, and violence is the rawest and ugliest expression of inhumanity. As stated in Chapter 6, when it comes to violence, a civil, smart society's stance must be that there is little to no tolerance for it.

At the same time, if we truly take into account the root causes and origins of most criminal behavior, then we must also take heed to not negatively aggravate the levers that foster them. Bad economic policies, racism, normalized anti-ex-prisoner sentiment, and derelict, overly punitive criminal justice policies and laws are all at the heart of the problem. The good news though, is that the problem is fixable. We fix it by systematically injecting higher levels of opportunity, compassion and fairness into our criminal justice systems and our society in general. We fix it by minimizing and eliminating as many roadblocks to real and meaningful rehabilitation and redemption as we can. For so long now, for the most part, we have been doing the exact opposite.

There are many forms of existing alternatives to incarceration, such as supervisory/probationary sentences, house arrest and home confinement, GPS monitoring, halfway houses, fines and fees, and community service. But if the ultimate goals are the reduction of incarceration and recidivism, then the argument can be made that these alternatives are being severely misused and underused in favor of imprisonment in too many cases. The general application of these programs should be retuned to assisting rehabilitative efforts more so than providing punitive surveillance, punishment or profit. **Humanity, compassion, fairness, and forgiveness have significant roles in corrections policy and efforts, and whenever possible, should outweigh the necessary element of punishment.** Otherwise, we as a nation are purposely not providing our citizenry their fullest chance for redemption, life correction, rehabilitation and success.

The misapplication and underuse of all these alternative programs make it seem, statistically, as if they can't really work as long-term deterrents to crime. On the surface, our unceasingly high recidivism rate appears to be the clear-cut evidence of that. But in this case, that evidence is revealed to be deceptive when analyzed in-depth. Sometimes, it's not what you do, it's how you do it. These alternatives could indeed work to reduce recidivism—when and if they are not being misused and underused. The big problem is that in today's anti-ex-prisoner culture, when these alternatives are utilized, the application is usually too punitive with stated goals that effectively amount to the stifling of the potential growth and correction of offenders. That is extremely counterproductive, to say the least. There is one looming, lingering fact that has to be accepted at some point, and it is that America cannot "punish" its way out of high crime rates and rampant recidivism. We keep trying but it is not possible. The more we try to do that, the longer high crime and high incarceration rates will remain a constant in our society—that is all but guaranteed.

Take a comparative look at a few situations that, for one of the authors of this book, are home-hitting examples of the typical misuse and misappropriation of incarceration vs. probation when it comes to nonviolent vs. violent offenses. Demico Boothe, a resident of Memphis, Tennessee, was sent to federal prison for ten years as an indigent teenager for a first-time offense of possession w/intent to sell an amount of crack cocaine that could fit in the palm of a hand. (This entire story is in the book *Why Are So Many Black Men in Prison?* by Demico Boothe.) Meanwhile,

another resident of Memphis, Keith Robinson, who
happened to be a church pastor whose family owns
an affluent funeral business in Memphis, physically
assaulted a sixty-eight-year-old woman on video, to
the tune of breaking her knee and collarbone and
kicking her after he had knocked her to the ground.
He was charged with domestic assault and received
probation for one year, with the assault conviction
being wiped off his record once he completed
probation due to him being a first-time offender.[99] As
a result, Robinson can still legally purchase firearms,
vote, obtain gainful employment and live wherever he
chooses, unlike Demico.

Another pair of similar situations, also hailing from
Memphis, TN, involve the brazen broad-day murder
of a rapper as well as another rapper who shot two
people in two separate situations within a two-month
time frame, all of which were caught on camera.
Adolph Thornton, also known as Young Dolph, was
recently gunned down in vicious fashion by two men,
one of whom previously had been convicted of
shooting three people in a bowling alley and had

served only six months in prison for it.[100] The other
Memphis rapper, Lontrell Williams AKA Pooh Shiesty,
was caught on surveillance video shooting a man after
robbing him and, after being released on bond, shot
another man while inside of a nightclub just a few
months later.[101] Pooh Shiesty was eventually given a
sweet deal and sentenced to less time for those
shootings than Demico Boothe was sentenced to for
possession of a small amount of drugs as a first-time
teenage offender.[102]

In all fairness, in those particular case comparisons,
shouldn't the teenage nonviolent first-time offender
have been the one that was eligible for a year of
probation and a cleared criminal record once it was
completed? Who do you think is more deserving to
go to prison for ten years; a nonviolent teenage first-
time offender who possessed a small amount of
drugs, or a full-grown man who beat up and severely
injured a female senior citizen? A nonviolent teenage
first-time offender, or a guy who went out to his car
and got a gun and came back into a bowling alley and
shot three people? A nonviolent teenage first-time

offender, or a guy who shot two people within two months, one of which was done while he was out on bond for the first shooting? I don't think most people would find these to be difficult questions to answer, yet the opposite is what actually happened in these cases. And it happens a lot. We could literally cite thousands of cases just like these if we intended this book to be a few thousand pages in volume. I'm sure that many of you have seen or heard of cases just like these. Cases where a petty thief steals $1500 worth of goods and gets big prison time, but in that same courtroom a white-collar criminal who stole one hundred times that amount got probation or significantly less prison time. This is typical, par for the course activity within our criminal justice systems. Oftentimes, money and connections can help deliver such divergent and imbalanced results, whereas indigence and lack of resources can literally be the cause of an innocent person doing significant time in jail or prison. But for the most part, these sort of things happen because of bad laws and legal procedures that allow for it.

If you ask us, being locked up is a cruel and unusual punishment for any living creature, especially human beings. Studies show that most people who have served time have PTSD, which no one ever talks about.[103] Therefore, our overall perspective is that people who do not need to be locked up should not be locked up. But if incarceration is to be utilized as a stiff tool of discouragement and punishment for certain criminal offenses, violent offenses are the most deserving of it, even for first-time offenses. Again, because America has such high and sustained levels of violent crime, a stronger message has to be sent out that lets it be known that all acts of violence are first priority when it comes to locking people up. We must hastily move away from the practice of building and filling up jails and prisons with millions of nonviolent people who don't really need or deserve to be there. We should eliminate most of the post-incarceration regiments for nonviolent ex-prisoners and primarily utilize those programs as front-end alternatives to incarceration for nonviolent offenders as well as post-incarceration supervisory tools for eligible violent offenders.

— — —

What this chapter deals with has a natural connection to what was discussed in Chapter 2. It involves a total refocusing of the tenets of pre-incarceration and post-incarceration programming, particularly for those with nonviolent offenses and/or short sentences. To be very clear, we believe the punishment for committing certain criminal offenses or being a repeat offender should be being put inside prison or jail for a specified amount of time. But anything more than that is just ancillary punishment that is either designed to make money or provide jobs for the public, while vindictively and unnecessarily making life harder for ex-prisoners. Additionally, as mentioned in Chapter 5, many studies have clearly shown that all the extra layers of post-incarceration regiments and punishments, though they function well at sending people back to prison, actually serve no real purpose in reducing crime or recidivism.[104] They actually do much more harm than good. They actively do more to *increase* crime and recidivism, again, by unnecessarily aggravating recidivism-causing levers within the fragilized lives of ex-prisoners. Therefore, they should all be reconfigured with some aspects of them being totally done away with. What should replace them is a more humane programmatic modus operandi and strategy. One that, among other things, operates from the principle of giving deserving citizens a real chance at redemption as well as the benefit of the doubt before meting out the harshest punishment, which is putting them behind bars.

10

Increase Training Requirements, Supervision, Accountability & Pay for Police Officers, Probationary & Correctional Staff

Police officers, probationary supervision staff, and prison and jail correctional staff are on the frontline when it comes to administering criminal justice and dealing with the criminal element. They are the ones within criminal justice systems with the most direct and meaningful contact with offenders, prisoners, and ex-prisoners. More so than judges, prosecutors, or lawmakers, they have an up close and personal purview of the causes and consequences within the lives of offenders, prisoners, and ex-prisoners. That means they have some of the most important roles in the collective effort to reduce crime and recidivism, seconded only by lawmakers and policymakers.

The citizens that hold these frontline positions have a great responsibility, and with great responsibility there should always be great accountability. And where there is great responsibility and accountability, there should be adequate compensation that is on par with those strict duty requirements and elevated standards. For quite some time in America, a big and visible problem has been that there has not been true accountability and supervision with respect to law enforcement agencies. Particularly within police departments but also with respect to correctional and probationary staff, who mostly work within an antiquated cultural framework that is anti-ex-offender, overly punitive, and that specializes in oppressive tactics and reincarcerating people on technical violations. Additionally, there has also not been proper and adequate training and compensation in these fields. So, although people like to continuously complain about all their shortcomings, if the axiom "you get what you pay for" was ever true, it is in this particular situation. Simply put, what's sorely needed are higher standards in conjunction with higher pay for police and probationary and correctional staff.

Though we have done our due diligence as far as research on this topic, we do not proclaim to be experts on police training. However, some of the issues at hand are well-known and well-documented. For one, there have always been heavy rifts and clashes between communities of color and police, often culminating in demonstrations, marches, and riots. The history of this goes back to the very beginning of policing in America and examples are too plentiful to count. From the terrible and largely untold experiences of dealing with the paddy rollers (the original American modernized policing system)[105] of the antebellum South; the Jim Crow police cartels that committed countless atrocities and provisioned the post-slavery convict leasing system;[106] the police enforcement of white supremacy, segregation, and redlining;[107] the police-involved Freedom Summer Murders;[108] the direct and peripheral involvement of the police in the assassinations of Dr. Martin Luther King Jr., Malcolm X, and dozens of Black Panthers;[109] the police brutality of Bloody Sunday in Selma;[110] the recorded beating of Rodney King; to the vicious murders of Fred Hampton, Laquan McDonald, Patrick Lyoya, Amadou Diallo, Michael Brown, Eric Garner, Tamir Rice, Walter Scott, Atatiana Jefferson, Philando Castile, Breonna Taylor, Jamarion Robinson, Kisha Michael, Marquintan Sandlin, Ahmaud Arbery, Oscar Grant, Quadry Sanders, Ezell Ford, Amir Locke and George Floyd. With literally countless other known and unknown incidents all along the way throughout the eras. It's clear that African-Americans have had and continue to have a totally different experience with American policing than white Americans. So have indigenous Americans, Latino Americans, and Asian Americans. It's high time that this reality is openly acknowledged, fully examined, and changed.

There has been a lot of discussion recently in the mainstream media concerning the need for improving the training, supervision, and accountability of police officers. Much of it has been reactionary unserious jabber, as it has always been extremely difficult to get pro-citizen policies and laws enacted when it comes to law enforcement.[111] This is because pro-citizen efforts purposely get misconstrued and mislabeled by politicized media as being anti-law enforcement. However, it seems that many citizens are becoming less willing to continuously accept idle and misleading talk, politicized surface solutions, and an unabated continuance of the status quo when it comes to this issue. There are now outcries and calls from citizens as well as a few new generation politicians to defund and/or restructure police forces,[112] based on them repeatedly showing a lack of tact, skill, and training in many recently publicized scenarios. In a few states, like Louisiana, Maryland, and Minnesota, some major reimagining and restructuring of police forces and police department protocol has actually happened as a result of some of their local and city governments taking action.[113]

We truly believe that, when it comes to police and law enforcement personnel in general, it all begins with the type of person that is recruited. In addition to defining what type of person is desirable, there should certainly be more of a redefining focus on what type of person is *not* desirable or fit for service in law enforcement. Many training experts agree with this.[114] Law enforcement officers have a lot of power when engaging with citizens, and power, if unchecked, is almost always abused by human beings. It doesn't matter if we're talking about democratic governments, monarchies, companies, or just the average everyday individual. The fact is, most people are flat-out incapable of properly handling having power over others, which involves large amounts self-control, a caring for humanity, and an inner affinity with the notion of fairness. Most people don't naturally possess all three of these qualities in great abundance, which is why it is necessary to have training and duty requirements along with multiple layers of supervision. But if recruitment and training processes are faulty to begin with, then as a result, supervision will be lacking and also complicit in the same faulty culture. The overall methodology of American policing has to be comprehensively redressed, beginning with staff recruitment and training.

Based on our observations, experience, and research on this issue, we can elaborate on two flaws within

police recruitment practices that directly affect the
effectiveness of law enforcement and undermines the
confidence that all Americans should have in them.
Before training even begins, the prototype recruits
that we should want for law enforcement should be
individuals who have life experience and people skills.
Thus, one of the problems is that too many of today's
recruits are coming directly out of college and have
never faced any complicated situations as adults or
learned how to relate to people from different
backgrounds.[115] Most of them have never personally
faced any violence or danger and don't have any
experience in dealing with it up close, other than a few
weeks of large-group simulated academy training.
Many of these recruits tend to be underprepared to
deal with the requirements and rigors of the law
enforcement profession and their lack of experience
and soft skills becomes dangerously apparent when
they are confronted with certain volatile situations.[116]

Then, on the other end of the recruitment spectrum,
you often have many nonspecialized recruits being
sought out and favored by police departments

because of their military combat experience. In other words, these departments want soldier-like, proven shooters and killers for their everyday police duty assignments.[117] These tend to be departments that historically have bad rapports with their constituency and much higher amounts of police shootings on record against civilians.[118] The ideology of "we want the soldiers, shooters, and killers" is a prioritized recruitment strategy of police departments that is inspired by militarist police trainers like Lt. Col. Dave Grossman, who has taught police training courses called "Killology" and "Bulletproof Warrior" since the late 1990's.[119] This ideology plays a big part in the militarization of police forces in America, which is about the utilization of military dogma, tactics, and equipment in urban environments. Police budgets have been substantially increased over the years in order to acquire these "tools" of law enforcement.[120] This militaristic posturing is not only overkill, it's further ingraining and indoctrinating an antagonistic, us vs. them culture into our police departments.

Nationally, police on average kill upwards of a

thousand people yearly, with at least a couple hundred of those being unarmed and a couple hundred more that were killed unnecessarily despite being armed with a weapon.[121] African-Americans are three times more likely to be killed by law enforcement than white Americans despite being 1.3 times more likely to be unarmed.[122] About 99% of killings by police do not result in criminal charges,[123] not because of the absence of guilt but more so because of white reluctance to hold the police accountable for violating the rights of mostly minority citizens.[124] As a result, it has become commonplace in America for the police to get away with killing unarmed citizens based on the most trivial of perceived threats like "I thought I saw a gun" or "he moved the wrong way" or even because a suspect resisted arrest or ran from them. African-Americans being shot in the back by police while fleeing has been normalized, and barely a few months go by now without hearing reports of such cases. Mostly, when these things occur, they are based on nothing more than fear, subjective paranoia, negligence and/or racism that are apparent because of bad recruitment practices and bad training.

So, although there is certainly a great need for law enforcement officers to be educated and capable of dealing with violent scenarios, there is also obviously a great need for officers to possess other prescribed character-based soft skills as well. The simplistic, two-pronged main recruitment strategy of today's police departments is one of the causative factors behind many of the problems that exist. Rather than mainly recruiting from two opposite ends of the experience and qualification spectrum, they should be looking more towards the middle. That is, recruiting more visibly unprejudiced and even-keeled people who have life experience and people skills. Attributing more weight to this kind of criteria within the recruitment process would expunge the majority of the issues that much of the citizenry has been complaining about for so long. The culture and accountability issues begin and end with recruitment and training, and most Americans actually agree that police culture needs to change and that police need to be held more accountable.[125]

While conducting research, we ventured to ask dozens of average, everyday people from all sorts of backgrounds and age groups for their input on police training based on any negative personal experiences they may have had. Most people that we approached had one or more experiences to share, especially African-Americans and Latinos. Among many other important things, most of them said that police training should teach recruits to:

- Have the utmost respect for the rights of all citizens
- Not routinely treat every person as a threat
- Not unnecessarily use intimidating behavior, language, or force
- Effectively use communication and decision-making skills
- Prioritize serving and protecting the community over looking for reasons to facilitate arrests
- Look for ways to de-escalate or end volatile situations without using deadly force, including learning to shoot to wound and disable (not kill) when appropriate

- Know and revere all relevant policies and laws relating to their duties and the rights of citizens

According to most of the citizens, these are very important communication, de-escalation, professional and humane methods that are all too often, if not routinely, not utilized when people come in contact with police officers. Again, we are not experts on police training, so we cannot say that some or all of these things aren't already being taught in police training academies. If you look at proclaimed police hiring requirements, they include simplistic or subjective character assessments with stated goals for desiring recruits with "good moral character, honesty, integrity, leadership, personal responsibility, dignity, respect and excellence."[126] However, we can certainly say that despite having these character assessments and activity directives in place, something is amiss as they're clearly not being utilized and adhered to enough. Which ultimately means they are not really compulsory requirements for employment with police departments. And they should be. A more compulsory national standard of behavior should be set based upon a much-improved methodology.

A supervisory part of that improved methodology should include civilian review boards. It is necessary to have civilian review boards that have the authority to prescribe and scrutinize all police actions and activity that involves citizens. They can also help get rid of the problem with peer and supervisory retaliation for whistleblowing as well as the "we've always done it this way" stubborn mentality that is pervasive within law enforcement governance circles.[127] The same way that the Constitution empowers civilians with direct oversight over the military,[128] civilians should have direct oversight power over their police departments more so than appointed or elected government-interested representatives and politicians. The same way that every major residential locality has a provincial government, courthouse, and jailhouse, every locality should also have a civilian police review board that works within a standardized national framework. Additionally, we need to find ways to limit police having to respond to calls that are better suited for other social service professionals, such as those dealing with mental health issues, nonviolent domestic/family issues, schools, homelessness, animal services and certain youth services.

An improved supervisory methodology, possibly including local, state, and national civilian review boards, is also severely needed within state juvenile systems. There are innumerous abuses that have seemingly been allowed to become commonplace within many if not most juvenile systems. The catchphrase "school-to-prison pipeline" is a colloquialism used to describe the effects of such abuses, which are often rooted in racist policies and practices by local officials and the lack of any real morality-based oversight or supervision. High-level oversight and supervision are too often only brought to bear on concerns about the economic aspects of juvenile court practices and the levels of facility occupancy. In other words, when it's about money being spent and beds being filled or not filled. Bad policies and practices are allowed to exist for decades within juvenile systems, creating situations where juveniles, some of whom are extremely young, are routinely mistreated, abused, traumatized, and unnecessarily imprisoned, oftentimes subjectively, with no recourse for redress.

The case of Kalief Browder is one example of this. This is a case that the rapper and businessman Jay-Z helped bring to the nation's attention. Kalief was an African-American juvenile that was held at the notoriously violent Rikers Island jail without trial for three years, two of those in solitary confinement, for allegedly stealing a backpack. He later committed suicide, which was likely due to having PTSD from his mistreatment by the New York juvenile system and his experiences on Rikers Island.[129] Another example of this was exposed in 2021, when ProPublica and Nashville Public Radio released a report entitled "Black Children Were Jailed for a Crime That Doesn't Exist. Almost Nothing Happened to the Adults in Charge."[130] This scathing report shows how one obviously racist juvenile court judge in Rutherford, Tennessee took it upon herself to wrongfully incarcerate over a thousand juveniles, most of whom were African-American, over nearly a twenty-year career. This culminated with the state having to pay eleven million dollars in a class action lawsuit but with no consequences for the judge and her enablers. These two examples are not isolated incidents; we could list hundreds and possibly thousands of examples of these sort of things occurring within juvenile correctional systems all across America.

The bottom line is, the status quo is not working, across the board. Hasn't been working for a very long time. The same hard shakeup and overhaul is needed within our juvenile correctional systems, our police departments, and our probationary and correctional staff. **America's approach to corrections needs brand new, comprehensive, far-reaching solutions to the problems that we face, not quick fixes or politicized retributive justice masquerading as real justice.** We are absolutely convinced that among those solutions are increased expectations and supervision and increased training and pay, which together would help attract and maintain candidates that are more likely to live up to higher standards.

Also, when it comes to training, studies show that
smaller classroom numbers tend to render better,
more capable studentry.[131] Thus, individual or small
group recruit training is preferable over large group
"cattle herd" training, which is what has been typical in
law enforcement. Person-to-person communication
and de-escalation skills are better absorbed with
small, live-subject, beginning-to-end reality-based
scenario training. At the end of the day, it is about
properly managing the motivation, activity, and
compensation of frontline law enforcement personnel.
Better training means a better ability to do the job,
while higher expectations and better pay mean a
higher respect and motivation for the job. A higher
respect and motivation for the job means a greater
likelihood of officers doing the job as expected, which
is all that citizens want and what they deserve from
their public servants.

Using a classic American movie for reference, here's
a relevant storyline that basically sums up the general
point of this chapter. In the film *Road House*,[132] Dalton,
a nightclub's prospective head bouncer played by

actor Patrick Swayze, demanded a significantly higher salary than the typical head bouncer because of his strict professionalism and high standards in doing the job. Once hired, he had one motto and requirement that he demanded of all the other bouncers that worked there. That motto was "Always be nice...until it's time to not be nice." This approach was something starkly different, completely opposite to the way all the town's club bouncers had always operated. Swayze's character emphasized this because he did not want an adversarial dynamic to exist between customers and bouncers unless it was warranted. He constantly reiterated that a bouncer's job was to "take out the trash" if necessary but to otherwise always be courteous to all patrons, even the ones that acted up. He told them to never forget that they were hired by the club to serve and protect club patrons in the first place, therefore all patrons were deserving of the utmost respect. Because of Dalton's influence, moral code, and style of leadership, that nightclub eventually became the safest and most successful nightclub in the entire town.

What Dalton realized is that the smartest way to solve a problem is to prevent it from becoming a problem in the first place, not reacting to it afterwards. His simple philosophy largely prevented the sort of issues that we've discussed in this chapter, and though police officers and probationary and correctional staff are not bouncers per se, their general mantra and attitude should be something similar to what his was. After all, and more so than for any other purpose, they are here to protect and serve the citizens of America. One cannot properly protect and serve those for whom one has little regard, respect, or affinity. Therefore, when it comes to law enforcement in general, it is not and never should be an us vs. them or them vs. us dynamic—it is simply us, and we must work together as Americans to make things better for us all.

References & Sources

1. U.S. Department of Justice, Bureau of Justice Statistics, 2021.

2. *Recidivism of Prisoners Released in 34 States in 2012: A 5-Year Follow-Up Period (2012–2017)*, special report by U.S. Department of Justice, Bureau of Justice Statistics, 2021.

3. *Recidivism of Prisoners Released in 34 States in 2012: A 5-Year Follow-Up Period (2012–2017)*, special report by U.S. Department of Justice, Bureau of Justice Statistics, 2021.

4. *Americans Don't Want to Defund the Police. Here's What They Do Want.*, article by William Saletan, Slate.com, 2021.

5. U.S. Department of Justice, Bureau of Justice Statistics, 2021.

6. *The Relationship between Economics and Crime*, report by ActForLibraries.org, 2017.

7. *Nelson Mandela quotes: A collection of memorable words from former South African president*, article by CBS News, CBSNews.com, 2013.

8. *History of Felony Disenfranchisement in America,* article by Kyle Johansen, Felonies.org, 2020; *Racism & Felony Disenfranchisement: An Intertwined History,* report by Erin Kelly, BrennanCenter.org, 2017.

9. *Can Trump Run for President from Prison?,* article by Sofia Andrade, Slate.com, 2021.

10. *Felons in Elected Office,* article by Emi Kolawole, FactCheck.org, 2008.

11. *History of Felony Disenfranchisement in America*, article report by Kyle Johansen, Felonies.org, 2020; *Locked Out: Felon Disenfranchisement and*

American Democracy, book by Jeff Manza & Christopher Uggen, Oxford University Press, 2008; *The Racist Roots of Denying Incarcerated People Their Right to Vote,* report by Jeffrey Robinson, ACLU.org, 2019; *American History, Race, and Prison,* report by Ruth Delaney, Ram Subramanian, Alison Shames & Nicholas Turner, Vera.org, 2022; *Racial Framing and Public Support for Ex-Felon Disenfranchisement,* Ole R. Holsti Prize winning course report by Michael Pelle, Duke University (DukeSpace.lib.Duke.edu), 2016.

12. U.S. Bureau of Labor Statistics, 2021; U.S. Census Bureau, 2021.

13. *Statement of Devah Pager, Professor of Sociology at Princeton University,* at meeting of November 20, 2008 – *Employment Discrimination Faced by Individuals with Arrest and Conviction Records,* U.S. Equal Employment Opportunity Commission, EEOC.gov.

14. U.S. Bureau of Labor Statistics, 2021.

15. *The Color of Justice: Racial and Ethnic Disparity in State Prisons,* article by Ashley Nellis, SentencingProject.org, 2021; *8 Facts You Should Know About the Criminal Justice System and People of Color,* article by Jamal Hagler, AmericanProgress.org, 2015; Bureau of Justice Statistics, 2022.

16. U.S. Bureau of Labor Statistics, 2021.

17. U.S. Bureau of Labor Statistics, 2021; PovertyUSA.org, 2021.

18. *Here's What The Racial Wealth Gap In America Looks Like Today,* article by Sarah Hansen, Forbes.com, 2020; *Racial and ethnic gaps in the U.S. persist on key demographic indicators,* article by Richard Fry, Jessie Bennett, and Amanda Barroso, PewResearch.org, 2021.

19. *Felony Disenfranchisement - The Lifelong Consequence,* article by Michael Diver, DiverLawFirm.com, 2020; *What Rights Do Convicted Felons Lose?,* TheLawDictionary.org, 2021; *Restrictions on Convicted Felons in Georgia,* article by Mackenzie Maxwell, LegalBeagle.com, 2018; *Rights of Convicted Felons in Texas,* article by Jessica Zimmer, LegalBeagle.com, 2021; *Tennessee Laws Regarding Felony Convictions,* article by Renee Kristi, J.D., LegalBeagle.com, 2019; *Doctors and the Law – How Can A Criminal Conviction Affect the Practice of Medicine?,* article by Adam H. Rosenblum, ESQ., RosenblumLaw.com, 2013.

References & Sources

20. Thirteenth Amendment, The United States Constitution.

21. *Mass Incarceration Timeline*, Preceden.com, 2022; *American History, Race, and Prison*, report by Ruth Delaney, Ram Subramanian, Alison Shames & Nicholas Turner, Vera.org, 2022; U.S. Department of Justice, Bureau of Justice Statistics, 2021.

22. *Marked: Race, Crime, and Finding Work in an Era of Mass Incarceration*, book by Devah Pager, University of Chicago Press, 2009.

23. *Jayson Williams Had to Live in Hotel After Prison, Couldn't Rent as a Felon*, interview of ex-basketball star Jayson Williams, VladTV.com, 2019.

24. *Republican efforts to restrict voting following the 2020 presidential election*, Wikipedia entry, 2021; *Same Old Jim Crow: Georgia voter law continues long history of disenfranchisement*, report by Southern Poverty Law Center, SPLCenter.org, 2021.

25. *No taxation without representation*, Wikipedia entry, 2022.

26. *Masterless Men: Poor Whites and Slavery in the Antebellum South*, book by Keri Leigh Merritt, Cambridge University Press, 2017; *Democrats & Jim Crow: A Century of Racist History the Democratic Party Prefers You'd Forget*, article by Sam Jacobs, LibertarianInstitute.org, 2020.

27. *What Percentage Of The Us Population Are Convicted Felons?*, Tntips.com, 2021; *Percentage of Americans with Felony Convictions Increases, Especially for Blacks*, article by Christopher Zoukis, PrisonLegalNews.org, 2018; *America's Invisible Felon Population: A Blind Spot in US National Statistics*, statement before the Joint Economic Committee On the Economic Impacts of the 2020 Census and Business Uses of Federal Data, by Dr. Nicholas Eberstadt, American Enterprise Institute, 2019.

28. *Ukrainian prisoners will be released from jail to fight in war*, article by Tori Richards, WashingtonExaminer.com, 2022.

29. *Patriotism Behind Bars: U.S. Prisons Aid the War Effort*, article by Kimberly Willig, Anna Griffin, and Gary Phillips, World War 2.0, 1942; *Exploring Military Service as an Alternative Sanction: Evidence From Inmates' Perspectives*, online thesis by Travis Wade Milburn, Eastern

Kentucky University (encompass.EKU.edu/etd/82), 2012; *Join the Army or Go to Jail?*, article by James Joyner, OutsideTheBeltway.com, 2006; *Which nations have armed prisoners and sent them to war?/ Was it ever possible to join the US military instead of going to prison for a crime?*, discussions by historians, History.StackExchange.com, 2012; *Dark Secret of the US Military – Neo-Nazis and Criminals Are Filling Its Ranks*, article by Matt Kennard, Alternet.org, 2012.

30. Synonym entries for *correctional* and *punitive*, Merriam-Webster.com.

31. *You Are The Reward*, article by Cesar Milan, CesarsWay.com, 2015.

32. *Psychological Well-being in Zoo Animals*, article by David Shepherdson and Kathy Carlstead, VeterianKey.com, 2020; *Keeper-Animal Interactions: Differences between the Behavior of Zoo Animals Affect Stockmanship*, article by Samantha J. Ward and Vicky Melfi, Journals.Plos.org, 2015; *What is Proper Stockmanship?*, article by Ann Adams and Tina Williams, HolisticManagement.org, 2017.

33. *Neurobiology of Sensation and Reward*, book by Jay A. Gottfried, CRC Press, 2019; *The Incentive Theory of Motivation*, article by Kendra Cherry, VeryWellMind.com, 2020; *Why Rewards-based Learning and Development Programs Work Better*, blog by Kristian F. Beloff, Blog.SellPro.net, 2021.

34. *Number of facilities and juvenile offenders by facility operation, United States, 2018*, Juvenile Residential Facility Census Databook: 2000-2018.

35. *What Are Juvenile Recidivism Rates and How Can They Be Reduced?*, Point Park University, Online.PointPark.edu, 2021.

36. *Locked Up for Being Poor: The Need for Bail Reform in Kentucky*, A Briefing Report of the Kentucky Advisory Committee to the U.S. Commission on Civil Rights, 2021.

37. *Locked Up for Being Poor: The Need for Bail Reform in Kentucky*, A Briefing Report of the Kentucky Advisory Committee to the U.S. Commission on Civil Rights, 2021.

38. *Locked Up for Being Poor: The Need for Bail Reform in Kentucky*, A Briefing Report of the Kentucky Advisory Committee to the U.S. Commission on Civil Rights, 2021.

References & Sources

39. *Suicide Risk Following Criminal Arrest,* article by Jennifer Piel, MD/JD, PsychiatricTimes.com, 2020.

40. *Locked Up for Being Poor: The Need for Bail Reform in Kentucky,* A Briefing Report of the Kentucky Advisory Committee to the U.S. Commission on Civil Rights, 2021.

41. *Justice Denied: The Harmful and Lasting Effects of Pretrial Detention,* article by Elizabeth Swavola and Léon Digard, Vera.org , 2019.

42. *How The For-Profit Prison Industry Keeps 460,000 Innocent People in Jail Every Day,* article by Luke Darby, GQ.com, 2019.

43. *Locked Up for Being Poor: The Need for Bail Reform in Kentucky,* A Briefing Report of the Kentucky Advisory Committee to the U.S. Commission on Civil Rights, 2021; *Suicide Risk Following Criminal Arrest,* article by Jennifer Piel, MD/JD, PsychiatricTimes.com, 2020; *The Cost Of Housing Inmates Who Can't Make Bail,* Talk of The Nation talk show w/ Neil Conan and Laura Sullivan, NPR.org, 2010.

44. *How the Bail Bond Industry Became a $2 Billion Business: Corporate insurance companies add a price tag to freedom and then make a profit,* article by Kayla James, GlobalCitizen.org, 2019; *Google Just Banished the For-Profit Bail Industry From Its Business Model. This Is Why You Should Care. 2.2 million people sit behind bars in the land of the free,* article by Kerry Kennedy, GlobalCitizen.org, 2018.

45. *New York Tried to Get Rid of Bail. Then the Backlash Came. A national movement stalled by backlash politics gets some new wind at its back,* article by Jamiles Lartey, Politico.com, 2020; *Illinois Becomes 1st State To Eliminate Cash Bail,* article by Cheryl Corley, NPR.org, 2021.

46. *Biden's order terminates federal private prison contracts. Here's what that means.,* article by Char Adams, NBCNews.com, 2021.

47. *Biden Is Holding as Many Immigrants in Private Prisons as Trump,* article by Eunice Cho, Newsweek.com, 2021.

48. *Biden Is Holding as Many Immigrants in Private Prisons as Trump,* article by Eunice Cho, Newsweek.com, 2021.

49. *Biden's key role in 1994 crime bill attacked by both Trump and Democrats,*

article by Kendell Karson, ABCNews.go.com, 2019.

50. *Biden Is Holding as Many Immigrants in Private Prisons as Trump*, article by Eunice Cho, Newsweek.com, 2021; *2021 Wrap-Up: Highlights From The Biden Administration's Historic Efforts To Reduce Gun Violence—Helping formerly incarcerated individuals successfully reenter their communities*, White House press release, Dec. 14, 2021.

51. *The Biden administration is using local governments to evade its promise to end use of private prisons—Criminal Justice and Immigration*, InThePublicInterest.org, 2021; *Remarks by President Biden at Signing of an Executive Order on Racial Equity*, The White House State Dining Room, January 26, 2021.

52. *A Brief History of America's Private Prison Industry*, article by Madison Pauly, MotherJones.com, 2016.

53. *The Biden Plan for Strengthening America's Commitment to Justice*, JoeBiden.com, 2019.

54. *Three Felonies A Day: How the Feds Target the Innocent*, book by Harvey Silvergate, Encounter Books, 2011; *30 Illegal Things Practically Everyone Has Done*, article by Alex Daniel, BestLifeOnline.com, 2018.

55. *The History of Welfare: An Introduction to the History of Welfare in America*, WelfareInfo.org, 2019.

56. *Prison Work Programs, Recidivism and Post-Release Employment*, report by Miriam Northcutt Bohmert, CrimeandJusticeResearchAlliance.org, 2020; *Research on Returning Offender Programs and Promising Practices*, report by David Muhlhausen, Ph.D., NIJ.ojp.gov, 2018; *Review: What Doesn't Work in Preventing and Reducing Juvenile Delinquency*, article by Sarah Krantz, Esq., CrimeFreeFuture.com, 2020; *Is Parole Ineffective or Effective in Curbing Recidivism?*, article by Audrey M. Saxton, AudreySaxton.com, 2014.

57. *Is it true that in the days of the "Old West", when a felon was released from prison he was given a horse and a rifle?*, Quora.com, 2021.

58. *Felony Gun Laws*, FelonyGuide.com, 2022.

59. *Can a Felon Own a Gun? 5 Loopholes in Federal Law*, article by Alana

Marie Burke, NewsMax.com, 2014; *Felony Gun Laws*, FelonyGuide.com, 2022.

60. *Public Believes Americans Have Right to Own Guns: Nearly three in four say Second Amendment guarantees this right*, article by Jeffrey M. Jones, Gallup.com, 2008; *The Second Amendment Is About an Individual Right, Not a Collective One*, article by Michael Marshall, Law.Virginia.edu, 2022.

61. U.S. Constitution, Bill of Rights, ratified December 15, 1791.

62. *District of Columbia v. Heller*, en.Wikipedia.org, 2022.

63. U.S. Department of Justice, 2022.

64. *How Many People In The U.S. Own Guns?*, article by Lisa Dunn, Wamu.org, 2020; *America's Complex Relationship With Guns*, article by Kim Parker, Juliana Horowitz, Ruth Igielnik, J. Baxter Oliphant and Anna Brown, PewResearch.org, 2017.

65. *Constitutional Carry at the State Level*, NationalGunRights.org, 2022; *States With Stand Your Ground Laws 2022*, WorldPopulationReview.com, 2022.

66. *Charges Dropped in Florida Convicted Felon Self Defense Case*, article by Eric Puryear, LearnAboutGuns.com, 2010; *SC: A Felon Has Rights to Self Defense*, article by Dean Weingarten, TheTruthAboutGuns.com, 2016; *Can a Convicted Felon Use a Handgun for Self Defense?*, article by Robinson Law Firm, GreenvilleCriminalDefenseLaw.com, 2020.

67. *In 30 states, a child can still legally own a rifle or shotgun*, article by Roberto A. Ferdman and Christopher Ingraham, WashingtonPost.com, 2014; *Minor in Possession of a Gun Laws*, LegalMatch.com, 2018; *Can a Felon Live with Someone Who Owns a Gun?*, WipeRecord.com, 2017.

68. *52 Shocking Gun Violence Statistics [2022 Update]*, SafeAtLast.co, 2022; *Background Checks Won't Stop Many Mass Shootings. We Need Them Anyway, Experts Say*, article by Tara Law, Time.com, 2019; *Deadliest Mass Shootings Are Often Preceded by Violence at Home*, article by Jackie Gu, Bloomberg.com, 2020; *Keeping guns away from potential mass shooters*, MSUToday.msu.edu, 2020; *History of Mass Shooters*, article by Sharon Shahid and Megan Duzor, Projects.VOANews.com, 2021.

69. *History of Mass Shooters*, article by Sharon Shahid and Megan Duzor, Projects.VOANews.com, 2021; *Gun Violence: Prediction, Prevention, and Policy*, American Psychological Association, APA.org, 2013; *Comparison of murderers with recidivists and first time incarcerated offenders from U.S. prisons on psychopathy and identity as a criminal: An exploratory analysis*, report by Nicole Sherretts, Daniel Boduszek, Agata Debowska, Dominic Willmott, ScienceDirect.com, 2017.

70. *Violence Prevention in Low- and Middle-Income Countries: Finding a Place on the Global Agenda: Workshop Summary*, Washington, DC: The National Academies, Institute of Medicine, 2008; *A Savage Order: How the World's Deadliest Countries Can Forge a Path to Security*, book by Rachel Kleinfeld, Pantheon, 2018; *Safest And Business-friendly Countries in The World*, article by The InCAP Desk, TheInCAP.com, 2022.

71. *Nonviolent Felons Shouldn't Lose Their Second Amendment Rights*, article by Ilya Shapiro and Matthew Larosiere, Cato.org, 2018; *Charges Dropped in Florida Convicted Felon Self Defense Case,* article by Eric Puryear, LearnAboutGuns.com, 2010; *FPC Supreme Court Brief: Non-Violent Felons Have Second Amendment Rights*; article by Duncan Johnson, Ammoland.com, 2019; *U.S. District Court: Some Felons Do Have Second Amendment Rights*, article by Dean Weingarten, TheTruthAboutGuns.com, 2018; *Amy Coney Barrett: I Own a Gun...and Non-Violent Felons Still Have Second Amendment Rights*, article by Dan Zimmerman, TheTruthAboutGuns.com, 2020.

72. *Race & Justice News: One-Third of Black Men Have Felony Convictions*, report by The Sentencing Project, SentencingProject.org, 2017; *Restorative Justice: An Alternative to Long Prison Sentences*, article by Katherine Beckett and Martina Kartman, Jsis.Washington.edu, 2018.

73. *The Disproportionate Share of Young Black Men Who Die By Gunfire*, article by Francesca Mirabile, TheTrace.org, 2016; *Black communities are disproportionately hurt by gun violence. We can't ignore them.*, essay by Nick Cotter, projects.PublicSource.org, 2022. *Black communities are most victimized by gun violence. Too often it's assumed we are to blame*, article by Gregory Jackson Jr., TheGuardian.com, 2022.

74. U.S. Census Bureau, 2022.

75. *Who's Using and Who's Doing Time: Incarceration, the War on Drugs, and Public Health*, article by Dr. Lisa D. Moore and Amy Elkavich,

References & Sources

NCBI.nlm.nih.gov, 2008; *Profile of Nonviolent Offenders Exiting State Prisons*, Bureau of Justice Statistics Fact Sheet, U.S. Department of Justice, 2004; *Justice system must address disparities of race, nonviolent offenses| Commentary*, article by John Jordan, OrlandoSentinel.com, 2021.

76. *States that Allow Conjugal Visits*, article by Debra C. England, CriminalDefenseLawyer.com, 2022.

77. *States that Allow Conjugal Visits*, article by Debra C. England, CriminalDefenseLawyer.com, 2022.

78. *Conjugal visit*, Wikipedia entry, en.Wikipedia.org, 2022; *Conjugal Visits in Prisons Discourse: Is it Even an Offender Rehabilitation Option in Africa?*, review article by Samson C. R. Kajawo, Malawi Prison Staff Training College, Advanced Journal of Social Science, PrisonLegalNews.org, 2021; *The Dark Origins of Conjugal Visits*, article by Alex Mayyasi, Priceonomics.com, 2015.

79. *How Do Conjugal Visits Work?*, article by Ijeoma Izuchukwu, Felonies.org, 2020; *How Conjugal Visits Work*, article by Victoria Cavaliere, Vocativ.com, 2016; *So What Are the Actual Rules with Conjugal Visits and How Did They Get Their Start?*, review article by Daven Hiskey, TodayIFoundOut.com, 2020. (Latter article cites an example of a prisoner convicted of assault still receiving conjugal visitation.)

80. *Pros and Cons of Conjugal Visits*, article by Alan Behrens, PositiveNegativeImpact.com, 2020.

81. *Reasons Prisoners Should Be Having More Sex*, article by Alex Mierjeski, archive.Attn.com, 2015; *Pros and cons of conjugal visits*, ProsanCons.com, 2019; *Conjugal Visits Aren't Just Real, They're Actually Really Great for Society*, article by Jill Harness, VistaCriminalLaw.com, 2021.

82. *Justice v. Profit (1619-Present)*, article by Kira Small '22, TheAcademyAdvocate.com, 2022.

83. *Crime & Justice in America: Punishment & Correction*, article by Erin Blake, Quizlet.com, 2022; *Prison Labor in the United States*, article by Kamau Littletree-Holston, Confluence.Gallatin.NYU.edu, 2019; *prison and punishment*, kids.Britannica.com, 2022; *The American Prison and the Normalization of Torture*, article by Bruce Franklin, HBruceFranklin.com, 2022.

84. *The Convict Leasing System: Slavery in its Worst Aspects*, article by Ellen Terrell, blogs.LOC.gov, 2021; *Convict leasing*, Wikipedia entry, 2022.

85. *The Convict Leasing System: Slavery in its Worst Aspects*, article by Ellen Terrell, blogs.LOC.gov, 2021; *Convict leasing*, Wikipedia entry, 2022.

86. *Mississippi State Penitentiary,* Wikipedia entry, 2022; *The Lasting Legacy of Parchman Farm, the Prison Modeled After a Slave Plantation*, article by Innocence Staff, InnocenceProject.org, 2020.

87. *Life (1999 film)*, Wikipedia entry, 2022.

88. *The Convict Leasing System: Slavery in its Worst Aspects*, article by Ellen Terrell, blogs.LOC.gov, 2021; *Convict leasing*, Wikipedia entry, 2022.

89. *UNICOR: Program Details*, BOP.gov, 2022; *Federal Prison Factories Kept Running as Coronavirus Spread*, article by Cary Aspinwall, Keri Blakinger and Joseph Neff, TheMarshallProject.org, 2020.

90. *UNICOR: Program Details*, BOP.gov, 2022.

91. *UNICOR: Program Details*, BOP.gov, 2022.

92. *Are Prison Commissaries Fair?*, article by Kate Wheeling, PSMag.com, 2018; *The High Costs of Phone Calls from Prison*, article by Cynthia Yue, EqualJusticeUnderLaw.org, 2020.

93. Federal Prison Industries, Inc., Fiscal Year 2021, Annual Management Report, November 12, 2021.

94. *Profiting off of Prison Labor*, BusinessReview.Berkeley.edu, 2020.

95. *Prison Industry Enhancement Certification Program (PIECP)*, BJA.OJP.gov, 2012.

96. *The Prison Index: Taking the Pulse of the Crime Control Industry (Section III: The Prison Economy)*, report by Peter Wagner, PrisonPolicy.org, 2003; *How much do incarcerated people earn in each state?*, article by Wendy Sawyer, PrisonPolicy.org, 2017.

97. *Forms of Punishment in the Criminal Justice System*, article by Lindsay Kramer, LegalBeagle.com, 2019; *Why we incarcerate: Punishment*, article

by Dr. Bruce Bayley, Corrections1.com, 2012; *What is the most common form of criminal sanction in the United States?*, AskingLot.com, 2022; *What is the purpose of criminal sanctions?*, AskingLot.com, 2020; *What Are the Four Sanctions Used to Punish Criminals?*, article by Knowledge Bombs, R4DN.com, 2021.

98. U.S. Department of Justice, 2022.

99. *Woman unhappy with pastor's plea deal after he pushed and kicked her*, news report by Greg Coy, Fox13Memphis.com, 2020.

100. *Young Dolph shooting suspect Justin Johnson in court for sex offender violation*, news report by Camille Connor, WLBT.com, 2022.

101. *Surveillance Video of Shootout Leads to Pooh Shiesty's Arrest*, article by Sha Be Allah, TheSource.com, 2021; *Rapper Pooh Shiesty Arrested for Allegedly Shooting Security Guard*, TMZ.com, 2021.

102. *Rapper Pooh Shiesty sentenced to more than 5 years on conspiracy charge*, article by Variety, NBCNews.com, 2022; *Why Are So Many Black Men in Prison?*, book by Demico Boothe, Full Surface Publishing LLC, 2007.

103. *Prisoner Post Traumatic Stress* article by Dr. Liji Thomas, News-Medical.net, 2019; *Prisoners at Higher Risk for PTSD*, article by Promises Behavioral Health / Dual Diagnosis, News and Research, Trauma & PTSD, PromisesBehavioralHealth.com, 2020.

104. *Prison Work Programs, Recidivism and Post-Release Employment*, report by Miriam Northcutt Bohmert, CrimeandJusticeResearchAlliance.org, 2020; *Research on Returning Offender Programs and Promising Practices*, report by David Muhlhausen, Ph.D., NIJ.ojp.gov, 2018; *Review: What Doesn't Work in Preventing and Reducing Juvenile Delinquency*, review article by Sarah Krantz, Esq., CrimeFreeFuture.com, 2020; *Is Parole Ineffective or Effective in Curbing Recidivism?*, article by Audrey M. Saxton, AudreySaxton.com, 2014.

105. *Slave patrol*, Wikipedia entry, 2022; *The Patty-Rollers Have Returned — but Did They Ever Really Leave?*, article by Vanessa Robinson, AnInjusticeMag.com, 2020.

106. *The History of Policing in the US and Its Impact on Americans Today*, article by Kala Bhattar, sites.UAB.edu, 2021; *Slavery by Another Name:*

The Re-Enslavement of Black Americans from the Civil War to World War II, book by Douglas A. Blackmon, Anchor Books, 2009.

107. *Slavery by Another Name: The Re-Enslavement of Black Americans from the Civil War to World War II*, book by Douglas A. Blackmon, Anchor Books, 2009; *The American System: How Police Enforce Segregation*, article by Grace Roberts, Dylan Horwitz, Evan Horowitz, & Cameron Tomaiko, storymaps.arcGIS.com, 2019.

108. *Murders of Chaney, Goodman, and Schwerner*, Wikipedia entry, 2022.

109. *Did You Know? US Gov't Found Guilty In Conspiracy To Assassinate Dr. Martin Luther King, Jr.*, article by Kirsten West Savali, NewsOne.com, 2021; *It's Been 52 Years, and Most Don't Know the FBI & Police Admitted Their Role in the Assassination of Dr. King*, article by Andrew Emett, TheFreeThoughtProject.com, 2017; *Researcher Fingers Jesse Jackson as Police-CIA Liaison in King Assassination*, article by Dr Stuart Jeanne Bramhall, StuartBramhall.WordPress.com, 2016; *Letter alleges FBI, police role in Malcolm X's death*, video on Reuter's YouTube channel, 2021; *Deathbed Letter From Former Cop Claims NYPD, FBI Helped Kill Malcolm X*, article by Ja'han Jones, HuffPost.com, 2021.

110. *Selma March*, article by Jeff Wallenfeldt, Britannica.com, 2021.

111. *As New Police Reform Laws Sweep Across the U.S., Some Ask: Are They Enough?*, article by Steve Eder, Michael H. Keller and Blacki Migliozzi, NYTimes.com, 2021; *One year later, George Floyd Justice in Policing Act has not passed despite Biden's promise*, article by Ericka Conant, AlDiaNews.com, 2021; *A discussion about how to reform policing.*, article moderated by Emily Bazelon, NYTimes.com, 2020.

112. *As New Police Reform Laws Sweep Across the U.S., Some Ask: Are They Enough?*, article by Steve Eder, Michael H. Keller and Blacki Migliozzi, NYTimes.com, 2021; *Defund the police*, Wikipedia entry, 2022.

113. *How Maryland's New Police Reform Bill Can Lead Us Forward*, article by Michael Lawson, LAUL.org, 2021; *New Louisiana abortion, policing, marijuana laws take effect*, article by Melinda Deslatte, APNews.com, 2021; *Minnesota governor signs police reform bill, critics say it doesn't go far enough*, article by Bradford Betz, FoxNews.com, 2020.

114. *A profession in crisis: Addressing recruitment and hiring practices in law*

enforcement, article by Nicole Cain, Police1.com, 2018; *Police education is broken. Can it be fixed?*, article by Caroline Preston, HechingerReport.org, 2020; *12 police recruitment ideas every agency should consider*, article by Greg Friese, MS/NRP, Police1.com, 2019; *Perspective: Characteristics of an Ideal Police Officer*, article by Larry E. Capps, M.S., leb.FBI.gov., 2014; *People Who Become Cops Tend to Have Authoritarian Personality Characteristics*, article by Chauncey DeVega and AlterNet, AlterNet.org, 2015; *5 principles to include in your hiring process to set your police agency apart*, article by Barry Reynolds, Police1.com, 2017.

115. *25 Ways to Make Police Training More Effective*, article by David Griffith, PoliceMag.com, 2015.

116. *Soft Skills You'll Need to Be a Successful Police Officer*, article by Timothy Roufa, TheBalanceCareers.com, 2019; *Five Critical Soft Skills When Evaluating Potential Officers*, LawEnforcementToday.com, 2017.

117. *Transitioning from Military Service to Law Enforcement*, article by TBS Staff, TheBestSchools.org, 2021; *Demilitarization of Police Means Disrupting the Army-to-Police Pipeline*, article by Suzanne Gordan and Steve Early, JacobinMag.com, 2021.

118. *Demilitarization of Police Means Disrupting the Army-to-Police Pipeline*, article by Suzanne Gordan and Steve Early, JacobinMag.com, 2021.

119. *I Learned to Think Like a "Warrior Cop"*, article by Justin Peters, Slate.com, 2020; *Who is Dave Grossman? Enforcement trainer tells cops sex after killing a human 'is best sex' in shocking video*, article by Sayantani Nath, MEAWW.com, 2021; *One of America's most popular police trainers is teaching officers how to kill*, article by Kelly McLaughlin, Insider.com, 2020.

120. *As U.S. crime rates dropped, local police spending soared*, article by Taylor Miller Thomas and Beatrice Jin, Politico.com, 2020; *Militarization fails to enhance police safety or reduce crime but may harm police reputation*, article by Jonathan Mummolo, PNAS.org, 2018; *The Militarization of America's Police: A Brief History*, article by Brian Miller, FEE.org, 2019; *Defund the Police, Defund Militarization*, article by Lindsay Koshgarian, NationalPriorities.org, 2020.

121. *2021 Police Violence Report*, PoliceViolenceReport.org.

122. *2021 Police Violence Report*, PoliceViolenceReport.org.

123. *2021 Police Violence Report*, PoliceViolenceReport.org.

124. *2021 Police Violence Report*, PoliceViolenceReport.org; *How can we enhance police accountability in the United States?*, article by Rashawn Ray, Brookings.edu, 2020; *Opinion: White people can compartmentalize police brutality. Black people don't have the luxury.*, article by Radley Balko, WashingtonPost.com, 2020; *10 things we know about race and policing in the U.S.*, article by Drew DeSilver, Michael Lipka and Dalia Fahmy, PewResearch.org, 2020; *Thousands of Complaints Do Little to Change Police Ways*, article by Shaila Dewan and Serge F. Kovaleski, NYTimes.com, 2020.

125. *Most Americans Say Policing Needs 'Major Changes'*, article by Steve Crabtree, news.Gallup.com, 2020.

126. *Police Employment*, MemphisTN.gov, 2022; *Careers with Lexington Police Department/Eligibility requirements*, LexingtonKy.gov, 2022; *Perspective: Characteristics of an Ideal Police Officer*, article by Larry E. Capps, M.S., leb.FBI.gov., 2014.

127. *How to defeat 'we've always done it this way' thinking in policing*, article by Police1 Staff, Police1.com, 2019; *New Perspectives in Policing: From Warriors to Guardians: Recommitting American Police Culture to Democratic Ideals*, report by Sue Rahr and Stephen K. Rice, Executive Session on Policing and Public Safety, Harvard Kennedy School/National Institute of Justice, OJP.gov, 2015.

128. *Why There Is Civilian Control of the Military and When That Tradition Began*, article by Luis Martinez, ABCNews.go.com, 2016.

129. *Kalief Browder*, Wikipedia entry, 2022; *Black Boys in Crisis: Kalief Browder and the Horrors of Incarceration*, article by Matthew Lynch, TheEDAdvocate.org (The Edvocate), 2017.

130. *Black Children Were Jailed for a Crime That Doesn't Exist. Almost Nothing Happened to the Adults in Charge.*, article by Meribah Knight (Nashville Public Radio) and Ken Armstrong (ProPublica), ProPublica.org, 2021.

131. *Benefits of a Smaller Class Size*, Fremont.edu, 2021; *5 Benefits of Small Group Learning*, article by Chameleon, GenieTutors.co.uk, 2016; *10*

benefits of small class sizes, article by EF Academy, EF.com, 2021.

132. *Road House (1989 film)*, Wikipedia entry, 2022.

The Right Key

Always

Unlocks the Lock